Guide to Foodservice Operations Management II

Mazy Publishing
Plattsburgh, NY
Copyright © 2014
ISBN 978-0-692-2362-1

No part of this publication may be reproduced, stored in a retrieval system, or transmitted in any form or by any means, electronic, mechanical, photocopying, recording, scanning, or otherwise, except as permitted under Section 107 and 108 of the 1976 United Stated Copyright Act without the prior written permission of the publisher.

The advice and strategies contained herein may not be suitable for your situation neither the publisher nor the author shall be held liable for any loss of profit or property damage.

Table of Contents

    Introduction………………………………..   1

Part 1- Samuel Ds Policy and Procedure

    Lab Safety…………………………………..   5
    Policies……………………………………...   7
    Conduct……………………………………..   8
    Dress Code………………………………….   9

Part 2 – Front of House – Dining Room

    Dining Room Procedures……………………   13
    Manager Responsibilities…………………….   15

Part 3 - Back of House - Kitchen

    Back of House Guidelines…………………..   17
    Manager Responsibilities…………………...   19

Part 4 –Recipes

    Bread………………………………………..   33
    Salad……………..…………………………..   34
    Dressing…………………………………….   35
    Butter, Croutons, Garnish…………………..   36
    Entrees……… …………………………….   39
    Vegetable…………………………………...   69
    Starch……………………………………….   77
    Dessert……………………………………...   85

Appendix
    Common Units of Measure………………...…   95
    Performance Evaluation……...……………..   97
    Mystery Shopper……………………………   101

Introduction

The experience that you will have in Samuel Ds should specifically enhance your understanding of the service and preparation component of restaurant operations. There are numerous steps and procedures involved in the process of delivering quality service to guests in a restaurant environment. We will utilize the service style typically found in a more upscale restaurant environment. Please understand that it is very important for the image of our program that you make every effort to deliver a quality dining experience for the guests visiting Samuel D's.

In order to have a comfortable and successful learning experience in this class you will need to come prepared to concentrate and exercise a fair amount of physical energy, especially compared to the typical course that you take in the HRTM program. Because of this fact it is important that you come to class well-rested and prepared to work hard, and also pay close attention to the details associated with proper dining room service. Please bring your manual as a resource each week.

We do not expect that you will master all of the skill sets that you will be taught, but instead that you have a measurable comprehension of the skills required in dining room operations. We understand that this is a laboratory learning experience so we are focused on learning rather than mastery of commercial dining operations. At the same time there is a certain level of urgency when we are open and serving the public to provide a professional and positive dining experience for all involved, and therefore requiring your concentration and attention to detail at all times.

Please feel free to ask questions at anytime. Also, please be punctual and follow the lab dress guidelines for the front of the house carefully. Attendance is essential for the class to operate efficiently. Personal hygiene and appearance are also very important in this course for obvious reasons. Again thank you for joining the course and we are looking forward to a productive learning experience.

Part 1

Policy and Procedure

Lab Safety – Why is it important?

Allowing untrained professionals into this course is an assumed risk the college has taken to allow you access to the best learning environment possible. While the college is willing to accept the risk we are responsible for making sure we have done due diligence by providing you with as much information as possible. Please take a moment to familiarize yourself with the facility, exits, and safety equipment.

Notify the instructor **immediately** if you or another student is involved in a lab accident. The following are areas where most accidents can occur.

Chemical Safety A Material Safety Data Sheet (MSDS) manual is located above the handwashing sink in the kitchen. The MSDS manual contains information about chemicals used in the facilities and first aid procedures should there be a chemical related accident.

Prevention Guidelines
> Store all chemicals in the designated areas, never around food.
> Never mix chemicals with anything.

Slips and Falls Slips and falls often cause injuries. Extreme caution should always be taken in the kitchen or on wet floor surfaces.

Prevention Guidelines
> Wear non-skid shoes
> Always keep containers covered when moving them.
> Always keep the floor clean and dry.
> Clean up spills immediately.
> Use wet floor signs after mopping.

Cuts Cuts are another common dining facility injury. Always use care when handling knives or sharp objects. There are bandages located in the restaurant kitchen.

Prevention Guidelines
> Never use damaged or defective equipment.
> Do not pick up broken glass with your hands, use a broom and/or dustpan.
> Keep knives sharpened and properly stored. Wash your own knife and do not place it in the dishwasher.

Burns Burns can be caused by heat or chemicals and are usually caused by improper handling procedures. Always exercise proper safety procedures when handling hot items or chemicals.

Prevention Guidelines
> Familiarize yourself with the equipment before use.
> Read labels before using chemicals if unsure.
> Never mix chemicals.
> Assume every pan is hot and handle with a **dry** towel.

Lifting Improper lifting of objects can result in several types of back injuries. Back injuries usually result in lost time and can become continuing problems for a lifetime.

> *Prevention Guidelines*
>
> Never attempt to lift very large or very heavy objects alone.
> Always lift with your legs, keeping your back straight while lifting.
> Do not carry loads bigger than you can handle.

Fire Safety Kitchen fire, although rare, is a possibility. Both the kitchen and the lab are equipped with automatic extinguishing systems. However, it is important to know how to locate and operate all of the extinguishing systems in both facilities.

> *Prevention Guidelines*
>
> Watch for accumulation of trash and linens.
> Use caution when handling flammable items such as sterno and gas lighters.
> Small fires should be extinguished with hand held extinguishers.
> If a fire is out of control, pull the red fire alarm box, call 911 and clear the building immediately.

Foodborne Illness The last thing a restaurant wants to worry about is making its patrons ill. To prevent this each individual must take responsibility to handle food safely.

> *Prevention Guidelines*
>
> Always handle food using proper sanitation techniques.
> Keep food covered and dated.
> Never allow food to reach the temperature danger zone.

AED

In the event that someone is having cardiac arrest there are two automated external defibrillators available for use within Sibley Hall. Please note the locations on the first day of class. If you are someone that is trained with this equipment or CPR please let your instructor know.

> *Prevention Guidelines*
>
> Prevention isn't possible in this case so being prepared is of utmost importance.

Taking the time to focus on prevention and preparedness before an incident occurs assists individuals in handling situations as well as showing due diligence. In addition to having these procedures in place you will also want to have documentation.

Policies

Food preparation and dining room service is a new experience for many students. To facilitate your work in the kitchen, we have prepared some guidelines of what the instructor will expect while you are working in the HRTM labs.

Sanitation
- Always wash hands before handling or preparing food.
- Keep hands away from face and hair while in the kitchen.
- Always step away from the work area while sneezing and coughing.
- Practice proper taste test procedures.

Beverages
- Open containers are forbidden by local code.
- You may bring a lidded water bottle that has a straw.
- All beverages shall be kept in the back hallway or the classroom.

Eating
- There is no eating allowed in work areas.
- Snacking in the store room or other work area is not permitted.
- Please eat before you come to the lab.
- Dinner will be provided at the end of the lab.

Supplies
- Measure accurately to avoid waste.
- Concentrate on tasks and avoid carelessness.
- Organize materials before beginning the task.
- Read recipes completely before beginning.

Product
- All food items should have a quality appearance and aroma.
- All food should have a pleasing taste and the appropriate texture.

Equipment
- Do not use equipment without instructions.
- Keep attention focused on the task in order to avoid injury.
- Clean equipment thoroughly after each use.
- Replace equipment where it belongs.

Emergencies
- DO NOT PANIC!!
- Notify instructor and follow instructions carefully.
- Being aware of procedures before they are needed is crucial for emergencies

Attendance and Punctuality

Attendance and punctuality are important to having success in the industry of business therefore we have set it as a priority for this class. The great leaders of business will tell you that if you simply "show up" that you are half way to success. The lab instructor has the final say in all lab related policies and grades!

Absences: You are expected to be at each lab, on time, and ready to work. The labs have a strict no absence policy. If you miss a lab session for ANY non-school related reason, there is no makeup and you will receive a zero for that lab day. If you intend to miss a lab session, you must still contact your instructor prior to your absence, so that we can reschedule around your absence. Contacting the instructor does not excuse you from the class. If you have a valid excuse from a physician please provide a detailed excuse slip.

School Function Absence: If you anticipate an absence from lab due to a school function (as described in the University of Plattsburgh Catalog), present written documentation from a school official to the instructor. The documentation should include the type of event that you will attend and the date of the absence. Absences for school functions may be made up without penalty and must be arranged no later than one week prior to the event.

Tardiness: If you arrive at lab after lab begins, one point will be deducted from your lab grade for every minute that you are late. The lab instructor will determine how many minutes you are late. Do not leave lab until you are dismissed by the instructor or you will receive a grade of zero for that lab session.

Attitude and Behavior

Students are to display; a positive attitude, teamwork, and common sense during lab experiences. This is important because we are serving the public and are evaluated by our customers at all times. A positive attitude and teamwork go hand-in-hand. Respect each individual this experience is a lot better and easier when everyone chooses to work together. Students are expected to display common courtesies toward their classmates during each lab session. Please refrain from profanity and other offensive or objectionable words in the lab. Failure to follow this policy will not only affect a student's grade but also may result in the student's removal from the class. The Classroom conduct Policy of the College will be enforced, this can be found at: http://www.plattsburgh.edu/studentlife/judicialcharges/collegeregulations.php

Alcohol and Drugs: Absolutely no consumption of alcoholic beverages or drugs on lab premises or before class will be allowed. Please be aware that we are working in a group setting in what can be a dangerous area. For your safety and others do not come to class impaired. Even over-the-counter medication can inhibit your ability to function. If either instructor suspects that you are impaired in any way we reserve the right to ask you to leave.

Smoking: is only permitted at the rear of the building (Sibley Hall) and only on breaks designated by the instructor. Please be aware that non-smokers are keenly aware of the smell of smoke. Especially if you are working in the front of the house you should have a mint before approaching customers.

Dress Code

A first impression is a lasting impression. We need don't need to say a word for people to make judgments. Whether this is right or wrong can be debated, however it is a fact that people make judgments based on looks. In the hospitality industry many times your employees won't have an opportunity to speak with guests and if they do it is only for a brief time. At Samuel Ds a server may interact with one or two tables but the guests are seeing every one of you. The back of the house is even further removed, we have no interaction with the guests but they are peering in the windows at us, they have no choice but to judge on appearance.

When you issue a uniform to your employees it allows you some control over what a customer sees. Whether everyone has the same uniform or different uniforms that tell where the employee works the consistency will benefit you as the employer.

Uniforms are also used to identify the brand. At Samuel Ds we have chosen excellence to define us. When you are wearing a Samuel Ds uniform you are showing that you are part of a team that prides itself on excellence. Even though we are not training chefs, wearing a chef's uniform has helped the community to see that not only do we cook food but that we take are serious about it. When people are only getting a quick glimpse you want to show them your best. A uniform is easier on the part of management as everyone wears the same thing. A dress code can become difficult to navigate for both the employees' and management as it isn't as clear cut.

Being properly dressed shows that you are committed to your own success as well as the company. There is much attention given to the first interview but your continued success will be in part be because of how you present yourself each day.

Samuel Ds Uniform

Front of the House
Black slacks. NO jeans, corduroys, low-riders, or stretchy pants.
White clean and **pressed** button down shirt. NO knits or any other kind of white shirt.
Black belt
Tie
Black socks
Black rubber soled shoes. NO sandals.
A black Samuel Ds apron
Plain white or nude undergarments
At least two pens

Back of the House
Black slacks. NO jeans, corduroys, or stretchy pants.
White clean chef's coat
Black socks
Black rubber soled shoes. NO sandals or high heels
Samuel Ds hat, hair must be restrained underneath your hat, long hair should be put up
Plain white t-shirt
No jewelry, wedding bands and small stud earrings acceptable
No fingernail polish, per health code
Solid white apron
Thermometer
Pen or pencil

Part 2

Dining Room

The Front of the House

Dining Room Procedures

The dining room procedures are designed to provide a consistent flow of service to the guests in the dining room at all times. These procedures are important to establish in any restaurant operation to coordinate, maintain, train, and evaluate the flow of service rendered to the guests at all times. These procedures can be modified depending on the level of formality that the dining room presents.

1. Approach the table and **welcome the guests** to Samuel D's –introduce yourself
2. Pour water **from the right**
3. Take the beverage order – **remove extra wine glasses** if necessary
4. Serve the beverage order and clear empty beverages from **the right** side when possible
5. Answer any questions on the menu and then ascertain guest salad dressing and entrée choices
6. **Take the entire meal order** starting with ladies first and go clockwise around the table
7. Enter salad dressing and entree selections into the POS
8. Serve the **bread**
9. **Serve** the salad **course from the left** when possible
10. Offer fresh ground pepper
11. **Notify expediter when salads have been cleared** and you are ready to pick up entrees
12. Make certain each guest has the appropriate utensils to eat their entrée before serving
13. **Serve entrees from the left** whenever possible – offer more beverages and make sure guest does not need anything else with meal
14. Check back to **ascertain satisfaction** within a few minutes after serving the dinner
Completely **clear the table** with the exception of active beverage ware and the center piece items
15. Offer coffee and dessert service - ask about cream for the coffee and enter dessert in POS after serving the coffee
16. Serve dessert and coffee – make certain the guest has proper dessert & coffee utensils
17. Offer refill for coffee
18. **Put 18% service fee** on the guest check
19. **Present check** and inform the guest that you will settle the check for them when they are ready
20. **Thank guest** for dining at Samuel D's

Other Server Policies

In providing the utmost service the details are crucial to not only making the guests happy but far exceeding their expectations. By following these simple but thoughtful policies guests will be delighted by the service.

- Carry at least 2 pens and a notepad
- Your comprehensive knowledge of all menu items including the wine is very important
- Greet guest within 30 seconds of sitting down
- Be attentive – fill water glasses when they are half empty
- Be polite and tactful
- Serve and clear all beverages from the right whenever possible
- Serve food from the left and clear from right when possible
- Hold all glasses by the stem only
- Parties of six or less serve all women first when possible
- Parties of more than six serve women to left of host (or any woman) and then serve others clockwise from her
- Do not reach across anyone
- When serving and clearing always use a tray
- Don't try to take as much as you can – looks sloppy and accidents can happen
- Minimize noise whenever possible; avoid chatting with students in the service area.
- Wait until each person is done eating before removing plates
- After the first course- take away dirty utensils. Do not have guests keep their fork or knife for the next course.
- Avoid touching the rims of glasses
- Please do not scrape plates in front of guests
- Don't leave the breadbasket empty on the table for the entire dinner; offer more, if they wish to have more fill it, if they do not clear it.
- Before serving the next course ensure that the table is clear of dirty dishes from first course.

Manager Responsibilities

The management in the front of the house is particularly difficult as you are managing your employees as well as guests. Reservations have to correspond with seating arrangements as well as server assignments. It is very important that the manager oversees the dining operations at all times making certain that students are following procedures correctly. There is a way of setting it and forgetting it.

Assign Opening and Closing Duties that are listed on the next pages
    Make sure that all duties are covered and understood
    Make certain all tasks are completed before the first guest arrives – assist if needed

Assign Tables
    Arrange the tables in the dining room
    Make up a model table
    Conduct a complete table check with servers
    Check for safety issues (loose chairs) – make certain there is adequate room for guests and servers to move about- table spacing is important

POS System
    Sign-in to register with instructor assistance
    Count money

Front Counter
    Have the reservation list ready
    Have the menus, wine lists and table assignments in place
    Prepare performance evaluation sheets with student names
    Open front door and adjust light level and music

Welcome Guest: (smile and welcome the guests)
    Ascertain the reservation name
    Hang coats if necessary
    Seat guests with a menu and wine list on the table
    Announce the name of their server and tell guest they will be there shortly
    Announce to student waiter their guests have arrived

Walk-ins
    Notify kitchen of walk-ins to assure there is adequate product, if we cannot accommodate the walk-in, apologize and suggest making a reservation for a future date

Management by Walking Around
    Keep a careful eye on front end tables to assist with beverages and water glasses, inform servers of anything that their tables might need

Guest Check
    Settle bills for guests – credit card *merchant copy* slip should be stapled to POS receipt and put into the register

End of Day
    Run Summary with and close out the credit card machine, count money and checks; reconcile totals with POS report

Closing
    Check to see that all closing duties are completed – assist as needed
    Be certain to obtain financial data needed to complete the post production report

Opening Server Responsibilities

Section One
Check beverage inventory: soda, beer, wine.
Prepare butter dishes and place in the refrigerator with milk and cream.
Set-up coffee station, do not brew coffee until 5:15.
Fill ice bucket and place on server counter with scoop at 5:15.
Assist in table set-up.

Section Two
Clean windows/doors with glass cleaner.
Wipe down server trays.
Bring out tray stands along with server trays, cover 10 trays with cloth napkins. Place trays and two tray stands in the kitchen for expediting.
Stock tea bags and make sure box is stocked as well.
Sweep server area, and place the floor mat in front of the coffee machine.
Assist in table set-up.

Section Three
Stock server alley with coffee cups, plates, tea pitchers, coffee pitchers, water pitchers and extra glassware.
Assist in table set-up.
Get the MP3 player and plug into sound system.

Section Four
Make sure sugar bowls are clean and filled with packets of sugar and variety of artificial sweetener.
Assist in table set-up, check for wobbly tables.

Section Five
Stock water and wine glasses.
Help fold napkins.
Polish salt and pepper shakers and make sure they are filled.
Assist in table set-up.

Section Six
Stock silverware and make certain there is back-up silverware.
Line the breadbaskets.
If available place butter rosettes in the cups. Place in freezer on a server tray; at 5:15 place the butter on the tables.
Adjust lighting for service.
Assist in table set-up.

Closing Server Responsibilities

Each night a restaurant closes it is best practice to have it all back to the way it was when everyone walked in. Assigning opening and closing side work is a way to break up the responsibilities so no one person is overwhelmed with work.

Section 1
Bring sodas from Beverage Cooler to either the walk-in cooler in kitchen or put out for family meal.
Bring coffee urns and filter holders to kitchen to be washed, bring them back to the server area.

Section 2
Wipe down server trays and place in kitchen on shelf neatly.
Clean front counter with Orange force for the granite, Ecoshine for the stainless steel counter.

Section 3
Sweep and mop server area
Sweep and mop front entrance.

Section 4
Put tables and chairs back in proper place for the morning operation

Section 5
Bring linen bag to the back of the kitchen near the recycling bin. Put out a fresh liner.

Section 6
Move the creamer counter back to the position for the morning operation.
Please plug in the milk dispenser and hot plate.

Everyone: Be sure you clean after yourself for family meal. Check the classroom before you leave.

Dining Room Layout

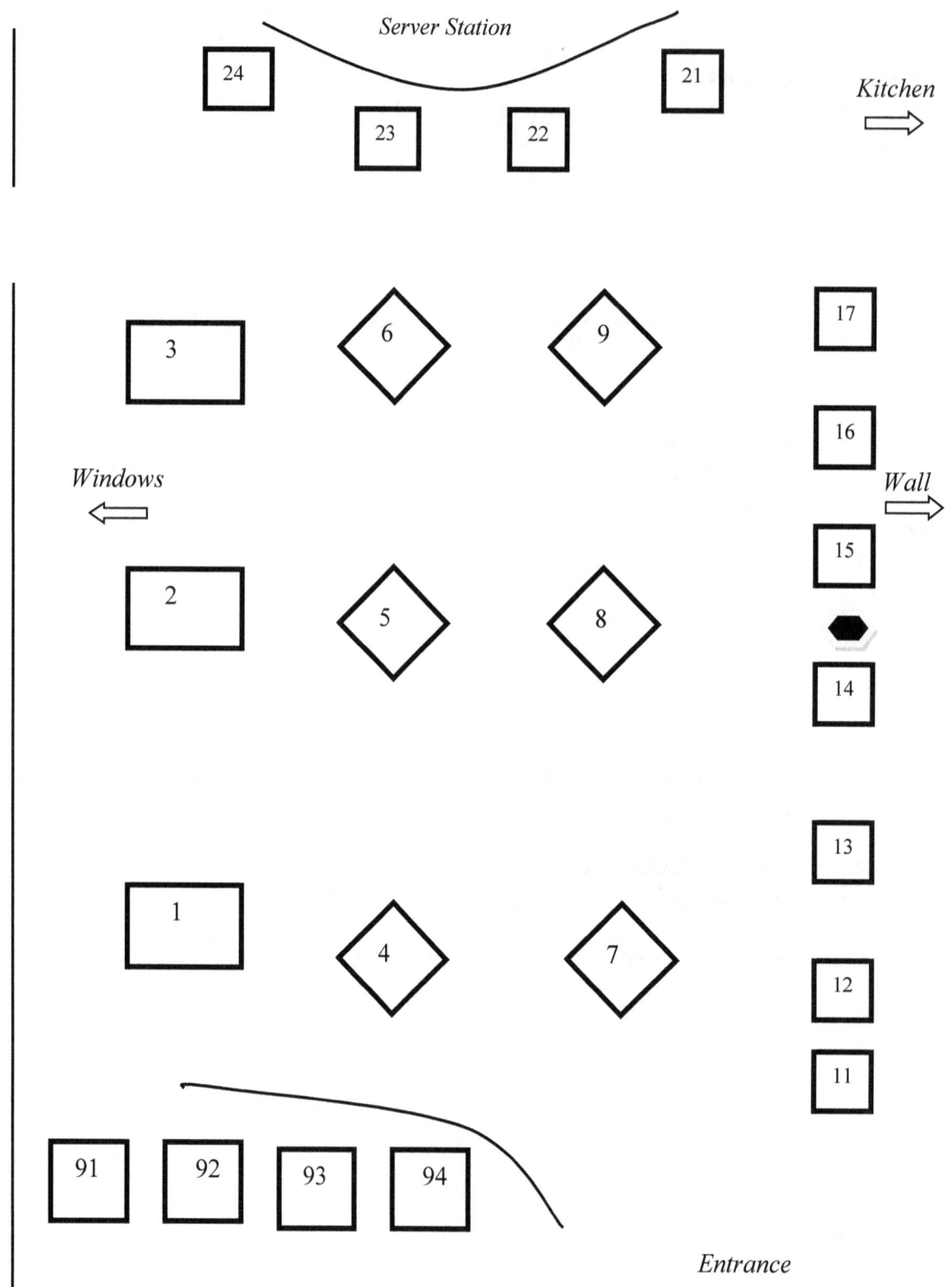

18

Payment Information

Handling of payment should be done with utmost care. Whether the payment be cash or credit the same attention to detail must be paid. Payment is just about the last transaction you will have with the guest it should be smooth and accurate.

Acceptable Payments:
Visa
MasterCard
American Express
Discover
Cash
Check (local)

Taking Payment
1. Press the table number (on the top right of the customer receipt)
2. Press the payment key
3. Enter payment amount and then press the payment type (i.e. cash, credit card, cardinal cash, gift certificate, etc.)

Payment by Credit Card

1. Put credit card strip down and with the customer's name facing the numerical key pad.
2. Slide card and wait for prompt
3. Type in the last four digits of number and press *enter* (green key)
4. Enter payment amount and press *enter* (green key)
5. Retain top *signed* copy, neatly staple signed copy to receipt

Sales Tax Policy

Non-alcohol food and beverage purchases paid for with State Funds are sales tax exempt Alcohol may not be purchased with State funds, so tax exemption on such purchases is moot Both food and beverage, including alcohol, paid with college Foundation funds is sales tax exempt. In all of the above cases, eventual payment must be directly from State or College Foundation funds. Purchases paid from personal funds that will be reimbursed to the purchaser by the State of College Foundation are not acceptable for tax exemption. Samuel D's is not to request a tax exempt certificate or exemption form for each individual transaction.

Part 3

Kitchen

The Back of the House

Kitchen Policies

The Kitchen or as we call it, the Back of the House, can be overwhelming at first but by following a few guidelines each student will be successful. The kitchen can be overwhelming because everything is new. By following a few simple guidelines we will all be on the same page and have the ability to focus on the task at hand.

To prevent injury please wash all knives you use in the three bay sink and immediately replace in proper spot.

Do not leave any sharp objects in the sink areas.

Drinks: you may bring water in a container that has a straw and lid. Open containers are against the health code.

Wash your hands frequently

Read through the recipe in its entirety before beginning

Sample food with a tasting spoon, knowing what the food tastes like is important. To gauge whether or not you need

Keep your workspace clean, cleaning as you go is important

If you burn a pot you must wash it yourself

When everyone chooses to work as a team rather than individually the work environment in any facet of the hospitality business is greatly improved. This classroom environment allows for mistakes, collaboration, and continued effort. Keep in mind that it is not a requirement to be a chef to take this class, only a student. A student must have a willingness to engage and participate in order to be open to the learning process.

Manager Responsibilities

Even if you are not the manager you should be reading this section, anticipating need helps you to excel. When you are the manager you will be the go to person when there are questions, use this checklist as a guide. Familiarize yourself with recipes and responsibilities before you set foot in the door to ensure that you are prepared. Following checklists will help you keep your management night organized. Delegate tasks to others; getting bogged down in doing all the details yourself prevents you from being an effective manager.

Before Service

Assign duties to students to ensure that all facets are complete.
Store any remaining food that might still be out from the delivery either in the walk-in or dry storage.
Fill sanitizer buckets and submerge a kitchen towel in each
Breakdown and remove debris from all cardboard boxes and put in the cardboard bin
Prepare mise en place for recipes
Assign breaks to students

During Service

Check that mise en place is done in its entirety.
Tell students to wash hands again and frequently throughout service
If using convection steamer should have the READY light on
Appropriate plates should be in the warmer
Serving utensils and gloves should be on the line
Clean kitchen towels for cleaning plates should be on the line
Fresh sanitizer bucket should be on the line
Garnish should be complete and ready to go
Warming lights should be on by 5:00 pm
Prepare dishwashing area
Sweep the line area

After Service

All food removed from prep sinks and make sure that they are wiped out
All hand sinks and backsplashes to hand sinks cleaned, and shined using Ecoshine
Floors swept
All countertops wiped down and sanitized
All cooking surfaces cleaned (ranges, backsplashes, steamer, kettles)
All shelves cleaned off
Garbage taken out to dumpster- make sure there is no debris left in the garbage can
Line garbage cans with new liners
Knives cleaned, dried, and in proper places
Fill paper towel rolls
Pick up all miscellaneous papers
Make sure all cardboard is clean, broken down, and put into the cardboard room
Turn off all equipment
Nothing left on the back table
Sweep and mop dry storage and walk in cooler
Floors Mopped – this should be the **last thing done** so as to prevent footprints
When done mopping rinse the mop heads.
All lights turned off

Use this checklist to ensure all tasks are completed

Job Assignments

Entrée _____

Entrée _____

Entrée _____

Bread _____

Starch _____

Vegetable _____

Dessert _____

Salad _____

Salad Dressing _____

Butter Rosettes _____

Garnish _____

Croutons _____

Dishes _____

Dishes _____

Sanitation Manager _____

Other _____

Cleaning Assignments

The BOH manager may assign the following as well as **other** cleaning duties you deem appropriate. Assign duties as you see the need: supervise the clean up process. The goal in a professional kitchen is to always leave it cleaner than you found it.

Mop_____

Mop_____

Assisting Dishwasher_____

Sweeping_____

Sweeping_____

Garbage (bring out to dumpster and reline cans)_____

Organize utensils (proper storage)_____

Ecoshine stainless steel surfaces_____

Sanitize all work surfaces_____

Return small equipment to proper storage_____

Organize china room_____

Purge expired ingredients from walk-in, sweep out and mop walk-in_____

Clean walls (backsplashes, near garbage cans)_____

Clean specific equipment used during the evening (alto-shaam, stoves, grill, etc._____

Family Meal

After service when both the FOH and BOH are done we get to eat. The BOH manager is responsible for overseeing that the meal is ready for the class to eat. Discuss with the FOH when an appropriate time for the class to eat will be. We wait until both the FOH and BOH are ready to eat. The BOH should be working right up until it is time to eat, after eating everyone is even more tired and clean up becomes difficult. Dinner is served to the students buffet style with everyone helping themselves.

Everyone should pitch in to help get ready or clean up before family meal. When we are serving ourselves we the goal is to have everything in place before everyone starts to line up. Assigning students to get some of the following items will help expedite the process. Ensure there is enough for everyone.

Plates_____

Silverware_____

Plastic cups from dry storage_____

Napkins from dry storage_____

One big salad made once all salads have gone out_____

Slice bread for us that doesn't need to be used for guests_____

Place serving tongs or spoons for each item on the buffet line_____

Entrees and sides finished cooking_____

Dessert - ensure that all dessert orders are in first_____

Condiments_____

Have waitstaff bring back open bottles of soda when appropriate_____

Bon Appetit!

Figure 1: Food Processor

> The following are some pictures of equipment and table setup for you to use as a reference.

Figure 2: Attachment used for shredding

Figure 3: Mixer with dough hook attachment

Figure 4: Mandoline and cut glove

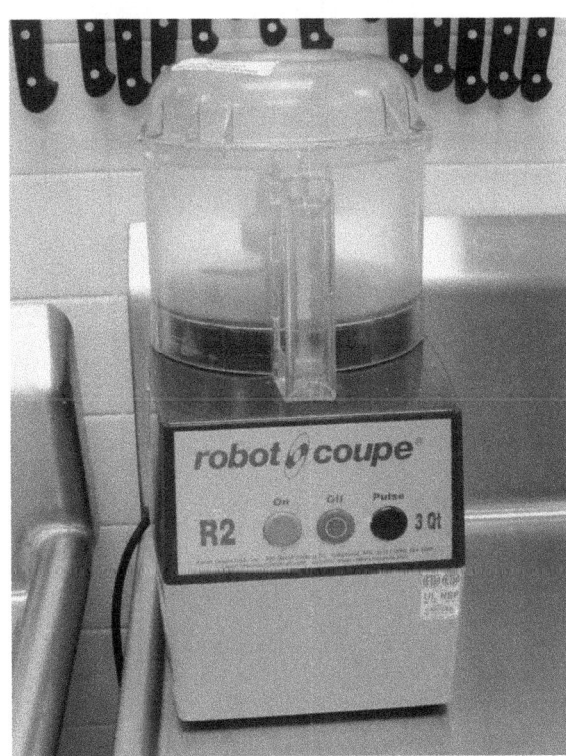

Figure 5: Food Processor for Salad Dressings

Figure 5: Table set for four

Figure 6: Place setting

Part 4

....

$$\left[\textit{Recipes} \right]$$

Samuel Ds Focaccia
Yield 60

....

87 oz. Water
¾ oz. Yeast
9 lbs. Bread flour – use scale to weigh
1 ½ oz Salt
1 oz. + Olive oil for brushing

Mix the tepid water and yeast, until the yeast is smooth. You will probably have to do this with a whisk. Put water and yeast mixture into the bowl. Add flour and salt.

Start the mixer on a low setting. Once it is combined you can increase the speed of the mixer.
Mix for about 12 minutes or until the dough cleans the side of the bowl.
Let rest for one hour. While the dough is resting prepare at least two toppings for the bread.

> **Toppings for Bread**:
> Parmesan cheese
> Olives
> Sauteed Onion
> Herbs

Flatten the dough into rounds, place on parchment covered sheetpan.
Brush with olive oil, dimple with fingertips.
Sprinkle on a smidge of salt.

Bake at 400 degrees F for about 5-7 minutes.
Bake all of the bread before service place on speed rack next to oven.
Slice the bread as needed for service. Do not slice the bread ahead of time for it will become dried out.

As a general rule serve:
4-5 slices   2 people
5-7 pieces   3 people
6-8 pieces   4 people
As the tables get larger you will be using two or more bread baskets per table.

Mise en place for service:
Gloves
Bread knife
White cutting board
Lined bread baskets (waiters will bring back)

Samuel Ds Salad
Yield 50-60
....

3 lbs. Lettuce Mix (3 lbs)
12-15 ea. Plum Tomatoes – 2 slices per plate
3-4 ea. Sliced red onion – 3 rings per plate
8-9 ea. Carrots, shredded

Garnish with house made croutons

Wash and rinse in the large orange salad spinner until leaves are mostly dry. Use the entire 3 lb. Bag of lettuce

Cut plum tomatoes into slices (you should get about 6-8 per tomato). Get an average of how many slices you are getting from each tomato. Make sure you have enough for each customer.

Slice the red onion on the mandoline, USE A CUT RESISTANT GLOVE. The slices should be very thin.

Shred the carrots in the robot coupe. (See me for instruction)

Place everything into the clear plastic containers and set up the salad bar.

Also put the dressings into the plastic containers and place in salad bar.

Mise en place for service: Gather all of these items before service begins

Gloves
Tongs
Ladles for dressing (smallest size)
Small gravy boats for dressing on the side
Salad plates chilled in the bottom of the salad bar.

Dressing:
Fill the smallest ladle ¾ full when giving dressing.

Samuel Ds Tomato Basil Vinaigrette
Yield 1 ½ qts.
……………………………………..
4 cups plum tomatoes, chopped seeded, divided
1 cup basil, fresh, coarsely chopped, divided
½ cup white vinegar
4 tbsp. Balsamic vinegar
2 tbsp. Dijon mustard
2ea. Garlic cloves
2 cups Olive oil
2 tsp. Pepper
2 tsp. Salt

Seed and coarsely chop the tomatoes
Remove stems from basil and discard, wash and pat dry the basil leaves.
Coarsley chop and pack into a 1 cup dry measuring cup. .
Coarsely chop the garlic.
Add these ingredients to food processor, blend for a couple of seconds.
Add the white wine vinegar, balsamic vinegar, Dijon mustard, and ½ cup of the olive oil.
Blend for another couple of seconds, until smooth.
Slowly stream in the remaining olive oil until well combined.
Season to taste with salt and pepper

Samuel Ds Creamy Gorgonzola
……………………………………..
¼ cup White wine vinegar
3 cups Gorgonzola cheese
8oz Sour cream
10 oz. greek plain yogurt
¼ cup mayonnaise
¾ cup Half & half
3 turns of the peppermill

Combine, vinegar, cheese, sour cream and mayonnaise, stir in heavy cream

Samuel Ds Dijon Vinaigrette
Yield 1 qt.
……………………………………
8 oz. White Vinegar
2 tsp. Salt
1 tsp pepper
4 oz. Oil
4 oz. Dijon mustard
½ cup honey
1 Tbsp. finely chopped parsley

Combine vinegar, mustard, oil, salt and pepper in blender until oil and vinegar are combined.
Stir in parsley

Samuel Ds Maitre d' Butter
....

2 lbs. butter (softened)
1/2 cup finely chopped parsley
1/16 of a tsp. of white pepper

If butter hasn't already been removed from the walk-in do so now, butter is best made when it is at room temperature
Wash, dry, then **finely** chop only the leaves of the parsley. Dry parsley with paper towel.
In the kitchen Aid mixer with the paddle attachment beat the butter until it is all the same consistency. Add the white pepper and parsley. Mix to combine thoroughly

Line 3 sheet pans with parchment paper. Using a star tip and plastic pastry bag; make single servings of butter.
Tip: for the paper to stay put apply a small amount of butter to underside of parchment paper.

This is a ready-to-eat item so you should wear gloves from start to finish.

Samuel Ds Croutons
Yield 1 sheet pan
....
2 loaves of focaccia, large dice
½ cup olive oil (+/-)
1 Tablespoon rosemary (diced, stems removed)
2 Tablespoons parsley (minced, stems removed)
1 teaspoon kosher salt
½ teaspoon coarsely ground black pepper

Prepare all ingredients place bread cubes in a large bowl sprinkle the ingredients over the cubes and toss gently. Add the olive oil slowly so you can adjust the amount. The goal is to cover each cube LIGHTLY with all of the ingredients. Don't over oil the cubes.

Bake on a piece of parchment at 350°F for 6-8 minutes or until the croutons are golden brown.

Samuel Ds Parsley Garnish
....
2 bunches of parsley

Using a chef knife, chop only the leaves of the parsley **extremely fine**.
Use rocking motion to move swiftly through all of the parsley. When you think it is fine enough chop it again. After you have checked to make sure it is fine enough.
Put the parsley in a paper towel and ring out all of the water from it.
Place in a small plastic container for service. Cover, refrigerate, place on line at time of service.

Note: There are many ways of doing garnish and this is a classic. Having the parsley small and dry allows the expediter more control of the garnish and the diner doesn't have to dodge or chew large parsley leaves. It is generally recommended to garnish with whatever is in the recipe so parsley doesn't always apply it is however a cheap, easy way to bring a plate together for a presentation together.

Entree

● ● ● ● ● ● ● ● ● ● ●

Balsamic and Herb Chicken with Goat Cheese Cream
Yield 20

....

20 chicken breasts- pounded
1 cup balsamic vinegar
½ cup olive oil
1 Tbsp kosher salt
1 Tbsp black pepper
½ oz fresh rosemary, chopped
¼ oz fresh thyme, chopped
2 Tbsp. fresh parsley, chopped

Pound the chicken so it has an even thickness. Place in 2 hotel pans. Combine vinegar, oil, salt and pepper; divide and pour over chicken. Refrigerate. Prepare herbs and set aside. Prepare goat cheese cream sauce and set aside.

Cream
4 oz. goat cheese
2 tbsp. heavy cream
¼ tsp. salt

Combine to make a smooth cream that can be put in a squeeze bottle.
Take chicken out of marinade, cover the chicken with the herbs.
Turn on grill- mark the chicken and put in the warmer. Cook chicken to an internal temperature of 165 F when an order is placed.

Melon Coconut Encrusted Chicken
Yield 30

....

30 chicken breasts
4 cups flaked coconut
2 cups bread crumbs
Eggs and flour as needed
2 honeydew melons (medium dice)
1 cantaloupe (medium dice)
Lime, zested and juiced
Olive oil TT
White wine vinegar TT
Salt and pepper to taste

Use standard breading procedure to bread the chicken with the coconut and panko bread crumbs.
Brown the chicken in a hot sauté pan, hold in warmer, at time of service continue cooking in the oven to an internal temperature of 165°F.
Combine melons and toss with olive oil, zest, and lime juice season to taste with salt and pepper. Top the chicken with the mixture.

Pecan Encrusted Stuffed Chicken Breast
Yield 20

………………………………………..
olive oil to grease foil
12 ounces thick sliced bacon, cooked crisp, drained and crumbled
20 (6-ounce) boneless skinless chicken breast halves, trimmed
12 ounces Roquefort cheese
2 teaspoon salt
2 teaspoon freshly ground black pepper
1 cup honey
10 tablespoons Dijon mustard
½ teaspoon cayenne pepper
2 cups flour
4 ½ cups finely crushed cornflakes
2 cups finely chopped pecans

Preheat the oven to 400 degrees F. Cover a small baking sheet with aluminum foil and lightly oil the foil with the olive oil. Set aside.

Working on a flat work surface, cut a deep pocket into the middle of each chicken breast half, cutting into 1 side and leaving a 1/2-inch margin all around the remaining edges. Divide the cheese and crumbled bacon evenly among the cavities in the chicken breast halves.

Season the chicken evenly on both sides with the salt and pepper.
In a small bowl, combine the honey, mustard, and cayenne and stir well.
Dredge each chicken in the flour then the honey mixture then coat with cornflake mixture.
Bake the chicken breasts on the prepared baking sheet and bake for 18 to 20 minutes, or until the chicken is cooked through 165 ° F and juices run clear when pierced with a sharp knife.

Almond Encrusted Chicken with Berry Balsamic Sauce
Yield 30

………………………………………………………..
5 cups fresh bread crumbs
4 cups crushed almonds
8 eggs
30 boneless chicken breast halves
1 cup of oil for sautéing

Sauce:
4 cups Berries
1 cup Balsamic vinegar
¼ - ½ cup sugar

Stir together breadcrumbs, almonds on a large plate. Whisk egg in small shallow bowl. Place plastic wrap over the chicken and place on yellow cutting board. Pound with flat side of meat mallet until the chicken is ½ inch thick. Sprinkle lightly with salt and pepper. Brush both sides with egg, then dredge the chicken on both sides in the breadcrumb mixture. Place the chicken in a ½ hotel pan and refrigerate until service.
When an order comes in you should, heat 2 tbsp. oil in a heavy large skillet over medium-high heat. Add chicken and cook until deep golden and cooked through. (About 4 minutes on each side)

Sundried Tomato Chicken
Yield 30
....
30 Chicken breasts, flattened
¼ cup olive oil (for sauté)
1 ½ cups sundried tomatoes, drained, chopped
1 cup white or blush wine
4 cups of chicken broth
5 shallots, thinly sliced
5 garlic cloves, minced
1 quart of cream
Salt and pepper, to taste
1 Tablespoon Paprika
2 cups Flour
Spinach as needed

Combine flour with paprika, salt, and pepper. Flatten chicken if needed, coat lightly each side of the chicken with flour mixture. Sauté the chicken on each side just until brown. Do not cook all the way through. Remove from heat and place in warmer covered tightly.
Make sauce – to some oil add shallots and garlic cook until translucent. Add tomatoes. Then add wine let simmer until some of the wine has softened the tomatoes just before service add the cream and let simmer for a bit. Adjust seasoning to taste.
Right before service or to order sauté the spinach in a bit of olive oil and salt and pepper.

Cook chicken to 165°F at time of service. At time of service place chicken on a bed of sautéed spinach and ladle sauce over top.

Chicken Chardonnay
Yield 20 Servings
....
20 chicken breasts
½ tsp. Salt
¼ tsp. Pepper
½ cup Flour , more as needed
2 lbs. Mushrooms
1 pint Chardonnay
1 ½ pints chicken stock
12 oz. Half and half
½ tsp. Dry mustard
1 ¼ lbs. Leeks, cut into triangles, blanched
Pound out the chicken breast, wash and pat dry, season with salt and pepper, and dredge in flour.
Sauté the chicken in olive oil until done. Remove the chicken and keep warm
Sauté the mushrooms.
Deglaze the pan with the wine; add the stock and dry mustard reduce by half.
Add the half and half and let simmer.
Add the leaks and let them heat through.
This sauce should be kept warm for service.

Chicken Provençal
Yield 10
……………………………….

10 breasts of chicken 7-8 oz
Salt, as needed
Pepper, as needed
Flour for dredging, as needed
Olive oil

Sauce
¼ oz garlic, minced
2 oz. capers
12 oz. Tomato concassé
10 oz. Dry white wine
24 oz. Demi glace
4 oz black olives, julienned
1 oz. Basil chiffonade

When ready to sauté blot to dry the surface of the chicken season with salt and pepper. Dredge lightly in flour. (Optional)
Heat a sauté pan, add the oil, and sauté the chicken 3-4 minutes per side or until done (165°F). Finish in a 350° F oven if necessary. Remove the chicken from the pan and keep warm while completing the sauce

Pour off the excess fat from the pan and add the garlic, sauté 30-40 seconds to release the aroma. Add the tomatoes and continue to sauté until any juices they release have cooked down. Add the wine to deglaze the pan and simmer until nearly cooked away.

Add the demiglace and any juices released by the chicken. Reduce to a good flavor and consistency.
Add olives, capers, and basil. Return to a simmer, adjust the seasoning with salt and pepper as needed.

Return the chicken to the pan and turn to coat with the sauce. Serve chicken on heated plates.

Brie Stuffed Suprême Chicken
Yield 24

....

24 suprême style chicken breasts
1 lb. brie
3 cups pecans
1 cup panko bread crumbs
3 cups flour
8 eggs
½ cup honey
4 eggs

Slice the brie into ¼ - ½ inch wedges. Set aside in refrigerator.
Portion out the pecans and dice.

Cut a slice into each of the chicken breasts – large enough to stuff in a wedge of brie.
Stuff the chicken.
Set up a "battering" station
Crack eggs and whisk together place in a half hotel pan; put pecan and panko together in a half hotel pan.

Chicken	Flour	Egg	Pecan/cornflake	Finished product

Refrigerate until needed.
Cook in 350 °F just before the chicken reaches 165°F drizzle with honey.
Garnish idea: honey butter

Fines Herbes Grilled Chicken
Yield 40

....

40 chicken breasts
1 oz rosemary
3 oz parsley
1 oz tarragon
1 oz thyme
1 oz chives
1 lb. butter

Remove the butter from the walk –in let sit at room temperature.
Chop all the herbs finely.   Combine ¼ of the herbs with the butter to make a compound butter. Roll in parchment paper and refrigerate. Combine the rest of the herbs with olive oil and coat the chicken. Grill the chicken until it is almost cooked all the way through. Cover with plastic wrap and aluminum foil.
Hold in the warming cabinet that should be 135°F.

Slice butter if it is cool.
Finish chicken in oven cook to an internal temperature of 165°F, serve with slice of compound butter.

Chicken with Pineapple Salsa
Yield 10
....

10 boneless chicken breasts
4 tsp. Chile powder
½ tsp. Salt
1 tbsp. oil
1 ½ lb pineapple, small dice
½ cup red onion, small dice
2 tbsp. cilantro or parsley
2 tbsp. lime juice
2 tsp. finely chopped jalapeno

Clean chicken, pat dry. Coat with chili powder and salt. This may be done ahead of time. Heat oil in a large ovenproof skillet. Add the chicken and cook over medium high heat until browned, about 2-3 minutes per side. Put skillet into oven. Bake at 350° F for 15 minutes or until the internal temperature reaches 165° F.

Combine pineapple, onion, cilantro, lime juice and jalapeno

Grilled Rosemary Lemon Chicken with Vidalia Onion Confit
Yield 30
....

30 Chicken breasts
10 lemons, sliced (need at least 30 slices)
2 sprigs rosemary, chopped coarsely
1 cup olive oil
½ cup balsamic vinegar
½ tsp. cumin
¼ tsp. cardamom
¼ tsp. coriander
½ tsp. ground black pepper
 Fresh thyme

Wash and pat dry the chicken. Set aside in the cooler. Combine olive oil, vinegar and seasonings. Marinate the chicken in the mixture in the cooler. While that is marinating; slice the lemons, toss in olive oil salt and pepper.
Then make the Vidalia onion confit- recipe follows.
Vidalia Onion Confit
5 onions, medium dice
2 Tbsp. butter.
Sauté the onions until they are soft and translucent. Hold in the warmer at which should be 135°F.
Preheat the grill, first grill all the lemons and set aside.
Grill the chicken to order; internal temperature should be 165° F.
Serve with lemon garnish and onion confit (rosemary)

Parmesan Chicken with Mixed Baby Greens
Yield 20
………………………………………………………….

3 cup fresh bread crumbs
2 ½ cups grated parmesan cheese
½ cup fresh, finely chopped parsley
5 eggs
1cup flour
Salt and pepper, to taste
20 boneless chicken breast halves
½ cup of olive oil
¼ white wine vinegar

2 lbs mixed baby greens

Stir together breadcrumbs, parmesan, and parsley on a large plate. Whisk egg in small shallow bowl. Place plastic wrap over the chicken and place on yellow cutting board. Pound with flat side of meat mallet until the chicken is ½ inch thick. Sprinkle lightly with salt and pepper.
Brush both sides with egg, then dredge the chicken on both sides in the breadcrumb mixture. Place the chicken in a ½ hotel pan and refrigerate.

You are going to brown the outside of the chicken only then hold until service.

Heat 2 tbsp. oil in a heavy large skillet over medium-high heat. Add chicken and brown on each side. Don't overcook it at this point or it will be dry for service.

Vinaigrette:
　　　　Combine olive oil, vinegar and a little salt and pepper. Set aside

When an order comes in continue cooking the chicken until it reaches an internal temperature of 165°F cook until deep golden and cooked through.

Put the baby greens on the plate, drizzle with vinaigrette, place chicken on top.

Chicken Marsala
Yield 40

……………………………..

Chicken:
40 Chicken breasts trimmed
2 cups flour
Salt and pepper to taste
Oil/butter for sautéing

Mix 2 cups flour with salt and pepper in a bowl. You are going to coat the chicken in this mixture before sautéing. (The flour will give it a nice golden brown color and richer texture) Pound the chicken with the flat side of a mallet. Putting plastic wrap over the chicken will help control the mess.

Dredge the chicken in the flour and then sauté them each side until they are golden brown. Do not cook the chicken all the way through yet. Place them in a hotel pan and cover them tightly and put in the warmer.

Sauce:
½ cup olive oil
2 onions, small dice
4 cloves garlic, minced
4 # mushrooms, sliced
1 ½ cups flour
4 cups marsala wine
12 cups beef stock
2 bay leaves
3 sprigs of thyme
Pepper, TT.
(depending up the wine and the stock you may already have enough salt in the sauce)
Add the olive oil to a large rondeau saucepan. When the oil is hot add the onions and garlic, once they are translucent (1-2 minutes no color to the onions) add the mushrooms. Sauté until the mushrooms are tender. At that time add the flour mixing it in thoroughly, cook for about 1 minute. Deglaze the pan with the marsala wine. Add beef stock, bay leaves, and thyme; cook until thick and the flavors are blended. If the flavor is there but the sauce isn't the consistency you want finish the sauce with monté au beurre (flour blended into butter). Remove bay leaf and thyme before serving.At time of service finish cooking chicken, pasta if called for, spoon sauce over entire plate.

Tuscan Chicken
Yield 45
....

Chicken
Pound chicken breasts until even
Season with salt and pepper
Parcook just as we have done in the past, put in warmer.

Topping:
10 lbs. Ricotta cheese
4 # spinach
3 cups sun-dried tomatoes
½ bunch of basil leaves (chiffonade)
1 tablespoon salt
 Pepper, to taste
1 cup Parmesan cheese
Sauté spinach just until wilted transfer to another pan and cool in walk-in.
Combine the rest of ingredients. Refrigerate.

Sauce
10 can Diced tomatoes
2 cans tomato paste
2 onions
Oregano
Basil
Olive oil
1 cup vodka
2 cups +/- heavy cream

Sweat the onions add diced tomatoes and tomato paste. Add seasonings and olive oil allow to simmer.
Use the immersion blender to get the sauce totally smooth.
Add heavy cream and vodka (see me for quantities to add).

Garnish
Basil chiffonade
Parmesan cheese

Asiago Chicken over Sautéed Spinach
Yield 20

....

3 cups panko bread crumbs
½ cup shredded parmesan cheese
2 cups shredded asiago
½ cup fresh, finely chopped parsley
1 cup flour
2 teaspoons salt
1 teaspoon pepper
1 tablespoon paprika
5 eggs
20 boneless chicken breast halves
½ cup of olive oil

3lb bag of baby spinach

Stir together breadcrumbs, parmesan, asiago and parsley in a ½ hotel pan. Whisk egg in small shallow bowl. Place plastic wrap over the chicken and place on yellow cutting board. Pound with flat side of meat mallet until the chicken is ½ inch thick. Season the flour with the salt, pepper, and paprika. Crack the eggs into a bowl and whisk together. Set up a typical "breading station". Dip the chicken in the flour, then the egg, then the cheese mixture. In a skillet generously oil the bottom and brown the chicken on both sides. Do not cook all the way through. Refrigerate. At time of service cook chicken in the oven at 350 °F until the internal temperature is 165°F.
Wash the spinach hold cold until an order comes in sauté the spinach with butter salt and pepper just until done.

Put the spinach on the plate place chicken over top, garnish.

Chicken with Provolone Prosciutto and Sage
Yield 70

....

6 qts. chicken stock
70 chicken breasts
70 thin slices of prosciutto
140 sage leaves (washed and dried)
70 very thin slices of provolone
      Olive oil for sautéing
6 Tablespoons of lemon zest
6 Tablespoons of lemon juice
TT Freshly cracked black pepper
1 cup olive oil

Boil broth until reduced to about half the volume.
Lightly pound each breast with flat side of mallet.
Cover smooth side of each breast with provolone, prosciutto and three sage leaves. Secure each leaf with a toothpick by weaving it through the chicken breast and each leaf.
Heat oil over a moderately high heat until hot but not smoking, then sauté breasts prosciutto side down until golden brown about 1 to 1 ½ minutes. Turn chicken over and sauté until brown on the other side about 2 –3 minutes reduce heat if necessary. When done cover with plastic wrap and put in warmer at 145 º F.

In the skillet (use a new one if there are burned bits of chicken on the bottom of pan) add lemon zest, juice, and reduced broth to pan. Whisk until reduced by half. Whisk in the 1 cup olive oil slowly adding less or more as needed. Season with cracked pepper.

Hold sauce on the line for service.
Finish cooking chicken in oven to 165º F.

Orange Glazed Duck
Yield 12

....

1 cup fresh orange juice
1 Tbsp. red wine
1 Tbsp. shallots, minced
¾ cup chicken broth
1/8 cup sugar

Sauté shallots before they brown add liquid ingredients then sugar. Let simmer. Taste, add ingredients as necessary.
Preheat oven to 350 F.
Cook the duck in convection oven for about 7 minutes. Brush on the glaze and continue cooking until done about 3 minutes.

Herbed Duck Breast with Pistachio Brie Cream
Yield 12
....

12 breasts of duck (skin attached)
16 oz. brie
½ cup pistachios, chopped finely
2 tablespoons heavy cream
1 bunch thyme, stems removed
1 bunch rosemary, stems removed, chopped finely
2 tablespoons, parsley, chopped finely, stems removed
1 tablespoon coarse salt
2 tsp. black pepper, freshly ground

Herb Rub
Combine the thyme, rosemary, parsley, salt, and pepper.

Duck
Thaw duck breasts and remove from package. Pat duck breast dry with paper towels.
Trim skin to the shape of the meat.

Score skin into 1/4 inch intervals. (Do not cut into breast meat). Rotate breast and score again, making a criss-cross pattern. Season with herb mixture you prepared.

Preheat a Teflon coated pan to low-medium low.

Place breast skin-side down for approximately 8-12 minutes or until fat is rendered and skin is crisp and brown. Low and slow is the way to go.

Turn breast over and cook 1-2 minutes. (Duck breast can be refrigerated at this point, then finished at a later time.) Place duck breasts in 400 degree F oven for 3-4 minutes. Let product rest 2-3 minutes before slicing. Final internal temperature should be 165 degrees

Pistachio Brie Cream
Scoop out the middle of the brie wheel, discard the rind, put the cheese in a bowl. Chop the pistachios until they are fine. Combine add the cream and adjust seasonings.
Refrigerate the mixture but be sure to remove it from the refrigerator before service as it will get rather firm.
To serve: place in a pastry bag with a star tip. After plating the duck, swirl a dollop of cream on top of the duck.

Herb Roasted Duck
Yield 15
……………………………………
1/2 oz finely chopped tarragon
¼ oz. finely chopped rosemary
½ oz. finely chopped parsley
½ oz. finely chopped herb of choice

Mix herbs together coat; stir into a ½ cup olive oil.
Cut the duck out of the packaging. Rub the duck with the herb mixture.
Roast in oven 14-20 minutes.
Onion confit
6 Vidalia onions, diced
½ tsp. firmly packed brown sugar
Salt and freshly ground pepper
¼ cup dry blush wine.
1 tbsp. fresh thyme
1 tbsp butter.

In a large sauté pan heat the butter, once hot add the onions and sugar season (LIGHTLY) with salt and pepper. Cook, stirring occasionally until the onions are soft (15-20 minutes). When just about done increase the heat to medium high; add the wine, cook stirring occasionally until the wine is reduced and the onions are a deep golden brown, 15-20 more minutes. Add the thyme and at this time add additional seasonings if required.

Cornish Game Hen
Yield 48

....

1 bunch chives, sliced thin
1 bunch rosemary, chopped
1 bunch thyme, taken off the stem
Combine the herbs. Mix with a bit of olive oil and salt. Rub the mixture over the Cornish game hen. Roast in oven 350 °F

Make the onion confit
6 vidalia onions, diced
½ tsp firmly packed brown sugar
Salt and pepper
¼ cup blush wine
1 tbsp. butter
In a large sauté pan heat the butter, one hot add the onions and sugar; season lightly with salt and pepper. Cook, stirring occasionally until the onions are soft. When just about done increase the heat to medium high; add the wine. Cook stirring occasionally until the wine is reduced and onions area golden brown.

Cornish Hens Maple Mustard Glaze
Yield 24

....

1 case of hens
1 ¼ cups maple syrup
½ lb. butter
¾ cup Dijon mustard
3 sprigs fresh thyme
½ tsp pepper
1 tablespoon salt

Preheat convection oven to 300°F.
Combine maple syrup, butter, Dijon mustard, and thyme and cook over low heat until butter melts, stirring until well combined.

Pat hens dry. Tie legs together to hold shape. Place in hotel pan. Season with salt and pepper. Brush with maple mixture. Roast until they reach 165°F. Baste occasionally with glaze. If they get too brown before they are done cover and return to oven.

Grilled Swordfish
Yield 12
....
8 oz swordfish steaks
2 teaspoons salt
2 teaspoons pepper
2 cloves garlic
Lime juice
Olive oil

Pesto
4 cups fresh basil, washed, patted dry
1 cup grated parmesan cheese
2/3 cup pine nuts, sunflower seeds may be substituted
2/3 cup of olive oil
Lime or lemon wedges for garnish

Take the swordfish out of plastic place in
Mince the garlic, combine with salt, pepper, olive oil, and lime let swordfish marinate in the mixture.
Make pesto in the food processor combine all ingredients pulse until well combined. Transfer to another container and refrigerate.
At time of service use a preheated grill. Grill 3-4 minutes on each side. Plate then spoon pesto over top.

Balsamic Glazed Salmon
Yield 12
....
1 ½ cup soy sauce
1 ½ cup balsamic vinegar
3T. sesame oil
3T. grated, peeled ginger
Salt and pepper, to taste
12 Salmon Steaks (1 inch thick)

Combine soy sauce, balsamic vinegar, sesame oil, and ginger; blend well. Pour this mixture into a saucepan and bring to a boil. Boil this about 5 minutes until it thickens and reduces. Coat the bottom of a roasting pan with oil and add the salmon steaks, sprinkling with salt and pepper. Roast the salmon in a 425 degree oven for about 7-8 minutes. Coat the salmon with the balsamic mixture and roast an additional 2-3 minutes.

Mango Salsa Mahi Mahi
Yield 10
....

3 cups mango, diced small (evenly)
1 cup red pepper, diced small
½ cup green pepper, diced small
¼ cup red onion, diced small
¼ cup Cilantro, chopped very small
4 Tbsp. fresh lime juice
1 Tbsp. olive oil

10 mahi mahi fillets

Prepare first six ingredients, combine. When ready to serve warm slightly, do not over heat or you will lose flavor and color.

Prepare mahi mahi with salt and pepper. To cook place in oven at 350°F. Cook for 8-10 minutes or until the internal temperature reaches 145°F.

Mango Salsa Salmon
Yield 10
....

3 cups mango, diced small (evenly)
1 cup red pepper, diced small
½ cup green pepper, diced small
¼ cup red onion, diced small
¼ cup parsley, chopped very small
4 Tbsp. fresh lime juice
1 Tbsp. olive oil
10 salmon filets

Prepare first six ingredients, combine. When ready to serve warm slightly, do not over heat or you will lose flavor and color.
Prepare salmon filets with salt and pepper. To cook place in oven at 325°F. Cook for 8-10 minutes or until the internal temperature reaches 145°F.

Roasted Red Pepper Sauce over Mahi Mahi
Yield 30

....

Sauce
6 ea. red peppers
1 ½ cups heavy cream
1/8 cup olive oil
2 ea. Cloves garlic
2 ea. Shallots

Wash the peppers, roast on the gas range until the outside blisters. Place in a bowl cover with plastic wrap. Let sit for 20 minutes or so.
Scrape off the skin and seeds. See me for technique tips.
Roughly chop the red peppers.
Finely dice shallots and garlic, sauté in olive oil until translucent (you don't want them to brown). Remove from heat. To that same pan add the heavy cream cook over medium heat just until it comes to a boil. Remove from heat. Combine, the red peppers, garlic, shallots, and heavy cream. (See me).

Mahi Mahi
Take the fish out of the bag and lightly salt and pepper the fish.
Refrigerate
Cook to 145°F at time of service.

Spinach
Just before service wilt the spinach in a large pan. You should do two batches during service. Place on plate just before serving.

Prosciutto-Wrapped Halibut with Sage Butter Sauce
Yield 20

....

10-12 lemons, sliced thinly, crosswise (rounds)
1 lemon, juiced
20 1-inch thick halibut fillets (6 oz)
60 sage leaves
60 thin slices of prosciutto

Juice the lemon, slice the lemons.

Season the fish with salt and pepper. Set two sage leave on top of each fillet and then wrap each fillet with a slice of prosciutto. The prosciutto should form a belt, enclosing the leaves. Lay wrapped fillets on top of lemon slices. Bake at 350°F until the fish reaches 145°F. Should be opaque and flaky at the thickest part; 12-15 minutes

While the fish is cooking, melt the butter in a skillet over medium heat. Add the remaining sage leaves and cook, turning once, until the leaves are crisp and butter begins to brown about 7 minutes. Add the lemon juice to the butter and season with salt and pepper to taste.

Maple Mustard Glazed Salmon
Yield 40
....

3 cups maple syrup
1 ½ cup whole grain mustard
2 Tbsp. cider vinegar
1 ½ Tbsp. chopped fresh thyme
1 tsp. kosher salt
1 tsp. fresh ground pepper
40 Salmon Steaks (1 inch thick) lightly salt them

Combine maple syrup, mustard, cider vinegar, thyme, salt, and pepper; blend well. Pour this mixture into a saucepan and bring to a boil. Boil this about 5 minutes until it thickens and reduces. Coat the bottom of a roasting pan with oil and add the salmon steaks, sprinkling with salt and pepper. Roast the salmon in a 425 degree oven for about 7-8 minutes. Coat the salmon with the mustard mixture and roast an additional 2-3 minutes.

Mediterranean Pasta with Shrimp
Yield 20
....

5 lbs.   Penne pasta
2 ea.   #10 can Tomato concasse/ diced tomatoes
1 cup   heavy cream (see instructor when adding)
1 cup   roasted red peppers or 3 each freshly roasted peppers
2 cups   Kalamata olives quartered – additional for garnish
3 cups   Artichoke hearts
¼ cup   Capers- additional for garnish
¼ cup   Feta cheese (per plate)
5 shrimp per plate

Garnish – Chopped olives, capers, feta

Roast the peppers on the grill
To make the sauce add diced tomatoes to large sauce pot (rondeau). Let simmer for half hour.
Chop peppers add to sauce.
Quarter kalamata olives
Cut artichokes into quarters.

Use the immersion blender in the sauce. Smooth out the large tomato chunks and red peppers. See instructor for consistency and adding the cream.
Add olives, artichoke hearts, and capers to sauce. Adjust flavorings.

Boil water for pasta

Cook pasta for 6 minutes
Portion into individual portions refrigerate
For service have the pot with pasta inserts filled with water and boiling at time of service.
When plating add ¼ cup crumbled feta cheese to plate, olives, and capers.

Shrimp Fettuccine Milano
Yield 12
....

2 lbs. uncooked fettuccine
60 (16/20 shrimp), peeled and deveined, tail on
3 garlic cloves, minced
3 tbsp. olive oil
3 lbs. Diced tomatoes
3 tbsp. basil, minced
1 ½ cups of heavy cream
¾ cup sliced green onions

Sauté shrimp and garlic in oil until shrimp are pink. Stir in tomatoes; simmer 5 minutes. Blend in cream and green onions. Heat through. Serve over hot cooked fettuccine.

Crunchy Fried Shrimp with Spicy Aioli
Yield 60
....

1. Peel and devein shrimp
2. Prepare the aioli
3. Prep the garnish
4. Fry shrimp right before service

Aioli
10 ½ cups mayonnaise
3 Tbsp. lemon juice (freshly juiced in juicer)
1 head/bulb garlic, minced finely
2 tsp. Cayenne pepper
1 Tbsp. Dijon mustard
When you have all ingredients in place see me before mixing them.
Whisk all ingredients together. Once combined see me to adjust seasonings.

Shrimp
4 cups cornmeal
1 Tbsp. Salt
2 tsp. cayenne pepper
12 lbs. shrimp
Mix cornmeal, salt and cayenne. Transfer a portion of mixture to another stainless steel bowl. Add 5-10 shrimp; toss to coat. In batches, so that the shrimp don't stick together add the shrimp to the fryer using the basket.
Garnish
Using the robot coupe with the blade attachment shred 3 heads of lettuce, hold in the walk-in until ready to use.

Crab Cakes and Shrimp
Yield 30 portions
………………………………..
Crab Cakes
5 lbs. crab meat (lump claw)
30 oz. heavy cream
2 red bell peppers, small dice
2 ea. Green bell peppers, small dice
5 bunches green onions, sliced
30 oz. fresh bread crumbs
5 Tbsp. Dijon mustard
5 ea. Eggs
1 tsp. worcestshire
1 tsp. Tabasco
5 eggs, slightly beaten

Reduce the heavy cream in a saucepan; bring to a boil and let simmer by approximately half.
Sauté the red and green peppers until tender.
Combine crab meat (leaving large pieces as big as you can), reduced cream, peppers, green onions, and approximately 1 lb. bread crumbs along with salt, pepper, mustard, worcestshire, Tabasco, and egg. Mix to combine all ingredients try to keep crab meat intact.
Using a mold, form the crab cakes.
Place the remaining bread crumbs in a hotel pan. Place the crab cakes in the hotel pan once they are formed pressing the breadcrumbs into the crab cakes.
Sauté crab cakes over medium heat. Be sure there is enough oil in the pan to cover the bottom completely. Sauté until brown on each side.
Check temperature and continue cooking in oven if need be.

Shrimp
90 shrimp
5 cloves garlic, diced
Salt and pepper to taste
Peel and devein the shrimp hold in the cooler until service. Cook each shrimp to order; put olive oil in sauté pan along with a bit of the garlic add the shrimp and salt and pepper to taste. Cook the shrimp until they are done (a light pink color and no longer translucent)

Remoulade for Shrimp and Crab Cakes
1 cup   Mayonnaise
¼ cup   Sour cream
          Chili powder
          Black pepper
1 Tsp.   Dijon mustard
          Tabasco sauce
1 Tbsp. lemon juice

Veal Piccata
Yield 20

....
20 each veal portions
1 Tbsp. salt
2 ½ tsp. black pepper
2 cups flour
½ lb. butter (+/-)
Canola Oil for sauté
1 white onion
4 cups white wine
5 garlic cloves, minced
5 lemons, juiced
¾ cup capers
½ bunch parsley, finely chopped

Add 3 tbsp butter to pan add garlic and diced onion. Cook until onion is translucent. Deglaze the pan with the wine and bring to a boil, scraping any browned bits, add the chicken stock, lemon juice, and capers cook until sauce is slightly thickened.

In a ½ hotel pan combine the flour and half the salt and all of pepper and stir. Quickly dredge the veal in the flour mixture. Season the veal with the rest of the salt (adjust as needed)

Heat the oil in a large skillet over medkium-high heat until very hot but not smoking. Add small amount of butter and sauté the veal in the butter. After you have browned each side add your sauce that you made earlier and the parsley. Cook until heated through.

Garnish ideas:
Sprig of Parsley
lemon

Veal Saltimbocca
12 Portions

....
3 pounds veal scaloppini, pounded to ¼ inch thickness
½ pound thinly sliced prosciutto
2 large bunch fresh sage
8 tbsp butter
2 cups dry white wine

Preheat oven to 250 F. Sprinkle veal on both sides with a small amount of salt and pepper. Top each with 1 prosciutto slice and 1 sage leave.
Add wine to pan drippings in skillet; cook over high heat until liquid is reduced by 1/3 scraping up browned bits, about 2 minutes. Add any juices from baking sheet. Swirl in remaining butter.

Melt 1 ½ tbsp. butter in heavy large skillet over high heat until foaming. Working in batches and adding more butter as needed, cook veal in single layer prosciutto side down, until brown, about 1 minute. Using a spatula, carefully turn veal over, keeping sage leaf intact. Cook until brown, about 1 minute longer. Transfer to rimmed baking sheet; keep warm until service.

Chocolate Espresso Rubbed Beef Tenderloin
Yield 25

……………………………………………………

6 tenderloins
1 cup espresso
¼ cup dutch process chocolate
1 tbsp. salt
2 tsp. fresh ground black pepper

Sauce:
2 Shallots, diced
4 tbsp., Butter
2 tbsp. olive oil
4 sprigs of thyme
1 tbsp. cracked peppercorns
1 magnum sized bottle of red wine
3 cups lower salt beef broth
1 tbsp. flour

Melt the butter and oil in a skillet over medium heat.
 Add the shallot and salt. Cook, stirring often, until soft and beginning to brown, about 6 minutes.
Add the thyme, peppercorns, and half of the wine.
Simmer briskly until the wine reduces about 10-15 minutes. Add the remaining wine and reduce again for another 10-12 minutes more. Add the beef broth and simmer until reduced by half, about 15 minutes. Strain through a fine sieve set over a 1 Gallon measuring cup, pressing lightly on the seasonings. Should have about 3 cups of liquid.

Steak Temperatures
....

Getting the proper steak temperature is an art form.
The following steak temperature guidelines can assist you.

Steak	Temperature Range
Rare	120-130°
Medium Rare	130-140°
Medium	140-150°
Medium Well	150°+
Well	160° not recommended

Grilling Times by Thickness

These are total cooking times. Divide in half for each side. Times are approximate and will vary.

Thickness	Rare	Medium	Well	Heat
1"	6-8	8-10	10-14	High
1 1/2"	8-10	10-12	12-16	High
2"	12-16	16-20	20-24	Medium

Marking the Steaks

To get the cross hatch grill marks on your steaks you must first have a hot grill. Preheat the grill before trying to cook steaks. Place the steak on the grill and leave it alone for at least 3 minutes. Using tongs turn the steak a quarter turn and leave it alone for another 2-3 minutes. When ready flip the steak on the other side and repeat steps. While the cross hatch appearance isn't imperative for a good tasting steak it does help to enhance the eye appeal.

Sauce

......

Bordelaise Sauce
Yield 15
....

3 tablespoons shallots, finely diced
1 sprig thyme
1 bay leaf
1/2 teaspoon peppercorns, crushed
1 1/4 cup red wine
1 3/4 cup beef stock
Salt and pepper, to taste
1 tablespoon butter

Combine the shallots, thyme, bay leaf, crushed peppercorns and wine in a saucepan.
Over medium heat, reduce about 90 percent, until the wine is the consistency of syrup, this will take about 10 minutes.
Add stock once reduced.
Cook the mixture until thick. You will know the sauce is thick enough when it evenly coats the back of your spoon, this is called napé. Strain and season with salt and pepper to taste, and swirl in butter off heat.

Beurre Blanc
Yield 1 qt.
....

1 oz	White wine
4 oz.	White wine vinegar
1 ½ tsp.	Salt
½ tsp.	White pepper
3 Tbsp.	Shallot, minced
2 lbs.	butter, chilled

Combine the white wine, white wine vinegar, salt, white pepper and shallot in a small saucepan. Reduce the mixture until approximately 2 tablespoons (30 ml) of liquid remain. If more than 2 tablespoons of liquid are allowed to remain, the resulting sauce will be too thin. For a thicker sauce, reduce the mixture.
Cut the butter into pieces approximately 1 ounce in weight. Over low heat, whisk in the butter a few pieces at a time, using the chilled butter to keep the sauce between 100° F and 120°F
Once all the butter has been incorporated, remove the saucepan from the heat. Strain through a chinois and hold the sauce at a temperature between 100°F and 130°F for service.

Horseradish Sauce
Yield 20 portions

....

2 cups Sour cream
¼ cup mayonnaise
1 bunch green onions (scallions)
¾ cup Horseradish
¼ tsp. Black Pepper
1 tsp. Salt
1 tsp. Lemon juice

Slice green onions, very thinly.
To sour cream add green onions, horseradish, pepper, salt, and lemon juice. Mix by hand, portion into small white ramekins for service.

Vegetable

. . . .

Asparagus
Yield 40

....
11 lbs. asparagus
½ cup olive oil
1 tbsp. salt
¾ tsp. ground pepper

Trim the ends of the asparagus using the rubber band as a guideline. Place the asparagus in a perforated hotel pan.
Turn on the steamer. Close to the time of service steam the asparagus for 5-6 minutes. Toss with olive oil, salt, and pepper.

Variations: Add mix-in such as sautéed mushrooms, red pepper, or lemon zest.

Balsamic Green Beans
Yield 40

....
10 lb. Green beans
8-10 small shallots
14 oz. Butter, softened
2 ½ cups balsamic vinegar

Wash beans, check the ends. Place in ½ slotted hotel pan.

Combine vinegar and shallots in heavy saucepan. Boil over medium heat until most vinegar is absorbed (about 2 tablespoons liquid should remain in pan), stirring frequently, about 6 minutes. Transfer mixture to small bowl; cool completely. Add butter; mix with fork until blended.

You will cook beans as you need them, right before service. Cook beans in convection steamer until crisp-tender, about 5 minutes. Combine beans and balsamic-shallot butter in large nonstick skillet. Toss over medium heat until beans are heated through, about 5 minutes. Season to taste with salt and pepper and serve.

Broccoli with Lemon
Yield 70

....
1 case plus 5 additional head of broccoli, trimmed and cut into spears
1 lb. butter
4 lemons, zested and juiced.
Salt and pepper to taste

Wash the broccoli and place spear in a slotted hotel pan.
Zest lemons and then juice them.
Measure the rest of your ingredients and have them available for service.
The broccoli will be cooked all at once right before we need it.
Turn on the steamer and check it once service has begun that the READY light is on.
Melt the butter by 6:00 pm. Cook broccoli by 6:15 pm.
Steam broccoli for 5-6 minutes.

Steamed Broccoli
Yield 35

....

1 case + more if needed broccoli
Butter
Salt and pepper

Wash
Cut broccoli into spears
Put into perforated hotel pans
Keep refrigerated until right before service.
One hour before service make sure the steamer is on and the READY light is on. Check the steamer again 20 minutes before you need to steam.
Steam the broccoli in batches.
Only steam what you need, when the broccoli sits on the steam table it quickly becomes brown.
Toss broccoli with melted butter and a small amount of salt and pepper.

When it is done bring over to the steam table.
Watch the line to see when more broccoli will be needed.

Roasted Broccoli
Yield 35

....

1 case Broccoli (14 heads)
1 cup olive oil, divided
5 ea. Garlic cloves, minced
2 Tbsp. Red pepper flakes
1 Tbsp. salt
2 tsp. black pepper

Preheat oven to 400 F.
Cut broccoli into larger florets.
1 hour before service, toss in 1 cup olive oil, sprinkle on pepper and salt.

Combine ¾ cup olive oil, garlic, and red pepper in bowl. Set aside.

Use at least 3 sheet pans, covered with parchment paper. Cover broccoli tightly with aluminum foil. Roast 10 minutes, check doneness.

If it looks about done, toss with garlic mixture uncover the pans and roast for 5-8 minutes. Watch it to make sure it doesn't get too dark.

Check seasoning, adjust if necessary.

Variation: substitute all or part with cauliflower

Glazed Carrots
Yield 40

....
12 oz. Butter
10 lb. Carrots
Sugar (+ or - 2 cups)
Salt
1teaspoon White Pepper
3cups Water
½ cup honey

Melt the butter in a sauté pan and add the carrots
Cover the pan and lightly sweat the carrots, about 2-3 minutes
Add the sugar, salt, pepper, water. Simmer.
Cover the pan tightly and cook over low heat until the carrots are almost done, about 2-3 minutes.
Remove the cover and continue to simmer until the cooking liquid reduces to a glaze about 2-3 more minutes. Stir in honey.

Green Beans Amandine
Yield 20

....
3 lbs. Green beans
8 oz. Slivered almonds
4 tbsp. butter
1 tsp. Pepper
2 tsp. Salt

Place almonds on a parchment covered sheet pan.
In a 350 degree oven toast the almonds for about 3-5 minutes or just until they are brown. Remember to set a timer because they burn very quickly.
Steam the green beans in the convection steamer. This must be turned on in advance before operating the steamer. Place the washed and trimmed green beans in a perforated hotel pan. Steam the beans for about 4 minutes. After 4 minutes if they need more try one more minute. In the meantime melt the butter.
When beans are finished toss them with the butter, almonds, salt, and pepper.

Snow Peas
Yield 30

....
5 lbs snow peas
5 Carrots, julienne
3 Red peppers, julienne
Salt
Pepper
Olive oil

Prep all ingredients hold. Right before service sauté in olive oil season with salt and pepper.

Butternut Squash with Maple Ginger and Cinnamon
Yield 60
....

45 lbs. butternut squash
1 cup maple syrup
¼ cup fresh ginger
1 Tbsp. cinnamon
2 tsp. salt
1 tsp. pepper
¼ lb. butter

Preheat oven to 350 F
Halve and seed the squash. Place cut sides up in a hotel pan, (like sizes together). Cover, roast for about 1 hour. Check it in 20 minutes to be sure that it isn't too brown.

Let cool to the touch. Scoop out flesh into a bowl. Mash squash slightly, while adding ginger, butter, syrup, and cinnamon. Add salt and pepper to taste.

Roasted Root Vegetables
Yield 20
....

3 lbs. carrots, peeled, cut into 1" pieces
2 lbs. parsnips, peeled, cut into 1" pieces
2 butternut squash, peeled, seeded, cut into 1" pieces
3 beets, peeled, cut into 1" pieces
3 ea. Red onion, cut into 1/8ths
1 garlic bulb with sectioned, cloves remaining peeled.
(Substitute with other root vegetables on hand)
1 tbsp. salt
2 tsp. pepper
½ tsp. dried thyme
Olive oil and ¼ cup honey to coat

Cut all the vegetables, coat with olive oil, honey, and seasonings. Roast in oven covered for 40 minutes, if they get too dark after 20 minutes cover and put back in oven.

Summer Squash
Yield 40
....
22 pounds squash, sliced on bias

Marinade,

2 pints oil
¼ cup white wine vinegar
5 oz. lemon juice
4 ea. cloves garlic

Combine all ingredients for marinade combine with squash.

Grill squash as needed.

Spring Corn
Yield 50
....
10 lbs. corn
4 bunches green onions, thinly sliced
2.5 lbs edamame
1 cup basil, finely chopped
½ lb. butter
1 Tbsp. salt
2 tsp. pepper

Chop the green onions and basil, set aside. At 4:45 melt butter in large rondeau, add edamame then the corn. Season with salt and pepper, when heated all the way through stir in green onions and basil. Remove from heat and place in half hotel pans.

Zucchini with Red Peppers
Yield 20
....
4 lbs.	Zucchini
1 ea.	Red pepper, finely diced
1 oz	Butter
tt	salt
tt	pepper

Slice zucchini on mandoline in an offset shape.
Sauté with butter and diced pepper until cooked through, season with salt and pepper.
Place in half hotel pan.

Roasted Cauliflower with Carrots
Yield 40
....
12 heads cauliflower
2 lbs. carrots, sliced
1 head garlic, peeled and coarsely minced
2 lemons, juiced
Olive oil 1 cup (+or-)
Course salt TT
Pepper TT
Parmesan cheese

 Cut cauliflower into florets.
Slice carrots on Robot coupe using slicing blade
Mince the garlic
Juice the lemons
Toss the carrots in olive oil place in 350 F oven roast until soft. Check in 10 minutes. When done hold in warmer at a minimum internal temperature of 135 F
Toss the cauliflower with lemon juice, garlic, salt and pepper
Closer to the time of dinner roast the cauliflower in 375 oven. Roast uncovered for about 20 minutes. Check frequently if it is too brown but not soft enough to poke with a fork tine place back in oven covered. Combine carrots and cauliflower
When done sprinkle with parmesan cheese

Acorn Squash with Cranberry-Orange Compote
Yield 50
....
21 lbs. acorn squash
1 ¾ lb. brown sugar
2 ½ lbs. butter
Salt and pepper, as needed
Quarter the squash and remove seeds. Place them cut side up on a baking sheet. Sprink the squash with sugar and dot with butter. Season each piece with a small amount of salt and pepper.
(If the squash fit in a hotel pan with the skin side down use that, if not use a parchment covered sheet pan)
Cover the squash.
Bake at 325 for about an hour, basting periodically

Cranberry Orange Compote
7 lbs. cranberries
2 ½ lbs. orange juice concentrate
Water, as needed
Sugar, 1 – 2 cups +
Zest of 12 oranges, blanched
Combine cranberries, orange juice, and enough water to barely cover the berries in a pan. Add sugar to taste. Simmer the berries over medium heat until they are softened and thickened. Add the orange zest.
(adapted from The Professional Chef, 7th edition)

Starch

Mashed Potatoes
Yield 10 portions
....
4 lb. Baking potatoes
2 ½ oz butter (room temperature)
5 oz. Milk
Salt, as needed
Pepper, as needed

Scrub, peel, and cut the potatoes into 1 inch pieces. Cook them in the steamer until they are very tender (tender enough to mash easily).

Strain, put in mixer add butter then the milk, once combined stir in salt and pepper.

Spoon onto heated plates.

Variation
Garlic Mashed Potatoes
Roast three heads of garlic in oven until very soft. Do this first. Add to mashed potatoes with butter.

Fingerling Potatoes
Yield 40
....
30 lbs. Potatoes
1 cup olive oil
1 oz rosemary
½ bunch parsley
tt salt
tt pepper

Scrub potatoes
Cut large ones in half or quarters

Chop rosemary
Chop parsley

Toss potatoes with olive oil and rosemary.

When potatoes are done toss with parsley

Lemon and Parsley Red Potatoes
Yield 25
....
Turn on steamer

20 lbs. red potatoes, washed, quartered
1 lb. Butter
¼ cup lemon zest
½ cup fresh lemon juice
1 ½ cups fresh parsley chopped finely
2 tbsp. salt   +/ -
1 tbsp. pepper +/-

Put potatoes in ½ perforated hotel pans. Don't over fill.
Steam potatoes in convection steamer, about 15 minutes.
In large rondeau combine butter, lemon zest, lemon juice, parsley, and potatoes, cook until heated through.
Flavor with salt and pepper.

Mashed Potatoes with Herbs
Yield 30
....
15 lbs.	Potatoes, peeled and quartered
28 oz.	Milk or cream, heated through
16 oz	Butter, melted
1 oz	Thyme, chopped finely
1 oz	Rosemary, chopped finely
1 oz	Chives, chopped finely
	Salt and pepper to taste

Turn on Steamer
After peeling and quartering potatoes, place in perforated hotel pans and steam for approximately 30 minutes.
While potatoes are steaming, heat the milk and butter and chop the herbs.

When potatoes are done immediately place in Hobart mixer with whip attachment, add milk, butter, and herbs. Place in warmed half hotel pans and cover immediately. Place in warmer.
Variation: cheese and chive mashed potatoes – omit herbs add chopped chives and shredded cheddar cheese

Parmesan Risotto
Yield 10

....

2 oz. Minced onions
2 oz. Butter
1 ½ oz. Butter (added at the end)
14 oz. Arborio Rice
5 ½ cups Chicken stock, hot
1 ½ cups white wine
salt, tt
pepper, tt
3 oz. Parmesan cheese

The white wine should be added to the stock as it heats up to a simmer.
Sweat the onions in the 2 oz. butter until softened and translucent, about 6-8 minutes.
Add the rice and mix thoroughly with the butter. Cook, stirring, until a toasted aroma arises, about 1 minute.
Add one third of the stock/wine mixture to the rice, and cook, stirring constantly, until the rice has absorbed the stock/wine mixture. Repeat, adding the remaining liquid in 2 more portions, allowing each to be absorbed before adding the next. Cook the risotto until the rice is tender but with a pleasing texture and most of the liquid is absorbed. The dish should be creamy. Season the risotto with the salt and pepper and stir in the parmesan cheese with the 1 ½ oz butter.

Potatoes Au Gratin
Yield 10

....

3 ¼ - low moisture yellow potatoes
24 oz. Milk
salt tt
pepper tt
5 oz grated cheddar cheese

Scrub the potatoes, peel, and remove any eyes or green spots. Slice very thinly on a mandoline. If done in advance, hold sliced potatoes in cold water to cover under refrigeration. Drain and blot dry before proceeding.
Combine the potatoes, milk, salt, and pepper. Simmer the potatoes over low heat until par-cooked, about 10 minutes.
Butter a hotel pan.
Layer the potatoes and milk in the pan, seasoning each layer. Top with the grated cheese.

Cover the pan with foil and bake the potatoes (in hot-water bath, if desired) at 350 F until tender, 45 minutes to 1 hour. Uncover and let the cheese brown lightly.

Roasted Potatoes with Garlic and Rosemary
Yield 20
………………………………………………..
10 lbs. Red bliss potatoes
2 ½ oz. Olive oil
2 ½ tbsp. minced garlic
2 ½ tbsp. rosemary
salt, as needed
pepper, as needed

Scrub and blot dry the potatoes. Cut into halves or quarters if desired. If potatoes are cut in advance hold them in cold water to prevent browning. Drain and blot dry before cooking.

Combine the oil, garlic, rosemary, salt, and pepper in a large bowl. Add the potatoes and roll or toss until they are evenly coated. You may have to use two bowls. Transfer to a sheet pan with parchment paper. Lightly coat the parchment with oil.

Bake in a 400°F oven until browned and tender enough to be easily pierced with a fork, about 40 minutes.

Roasted Sweet Potatoes
Yield 50
………………………….
40 lbs. sweet potatoes, peeled and cut into ½ inch cubes
2 lbs. butter, melted
2 Tbsp. salt
1 Tbsp. pepper
3 cups water
1 ¼ cup sugar
¾ cup freshly squeezed lime juice
2 Tbsp. lime zest, finely grated
1 bunch fresh chives, finely chopped
2 tsp. cayenne

Preheat oven to 375° F.
Toss the potatoes with butter, salt, and pepper in a bowl. (You might have to do this in two or three steps because of the amount of potatoes). Make sure all the potatoes are covered then spread in one layer into a hotel pan (use as many as needed). Roast covered for 10 minutes. Remove lids, rotate pans and roast additional time until the potatoes are tender 7- 15 minutes more.

While potatoes are roasting bring water, sugar, and lime juice to a boil in a pan, stirring until the sugar dissolves, then simmer for 5 minutes. Toss the potatoes with syrup, lime zest, chives, and cayenne pepper.

Brown Rice Pilaf
Yield 20
....
18 oz. brown rice (weigh on scale)
3 oz. vegetable oil (canola)
2 oz. minced onion
8 ½ cups chicken stock (hot)
4 ea. bay leaves
4 ea. Sprigs of fresh thyme (optional)
1 cup green pepper (small dice)
1 cup carrot (small dice)
1 cup orzo (optional)
2 tsp. salt
1 tsp. pepper

Heat the oil in a large rondeau on medium heat. Add the onion and sweat, stirring frequently, until they are soft and translucent. About 6 minutes

Add the rice and sauté, stirring frequently, until coated with oil and heated through. Add the heated stock to the rice. Bring to a simmer, stirring the rice once or twice to prevent it from clumping. COVER THE POT with a lid.

Add the bay leaf, thyme, salt, and pepper. Cover the pot and let simmer over a low heat. Brown rice takes longer to cook than white rice. Simmer for about 35 minutes or until all of the liquid is absorbed.

While the rice is simmering cook the pepper and carrot until they are soft. Stir into the rice once it is done cooking.

Brown Rice Pilaf with Pecans and Scallions
Yield 80

....

7 lbs. brown rice
12 oz butter
1 lb. onions, minced
2 ½ Gallons chicken stock
Bouquet garni, thyme, bay leaf, garlic, parsley stems
Salt and pepper, as needed
1 lb. pecans, chopped, toasted
1 lb. scallions, sliced thin

Use two pans to make the rice.
Heat the butter in a pot over medium heat, add the onion and sweat, stirring frequently until translucent. Add the heated stock to the rice. Bring to a simmer, stirring the rice once or twice to prevent it from clumping.
Add the bouquet garni, salt, and pepper. Cover the pot and let simmer on a very low flame. Cook until grains are tender, about 45 minutes to an hour.
When done, fold in pecans and scallions.

This can be put in a full hotel pan and put in the warmer until service. At time of service the rice will go into the steam table.

Dessert

· · · · · · · · ·

Molten Chocolate Cake
Yield 70

....
Cake
4 ½ lbs butter (cut into 1-inch pieces)
½ lb butter, for molds
¾ cup all purpose flour
¼ cup all purpose flour, for molds
4.5 lbs. chocolate, chopped
36 eggs
36 egg yolks
4 ½ cups granulated sugar

Raspberry sauce
6 cups raspberries
2 cups sugar
Heat to a boil let simmer, strain. refrigerate
Heat convection oven to 400. Butter and lightly flour 70 aluminum molds. Tap out excess flour. Use a double boiler set over hot (not boiling) water to heat the butter and chocolate together until the chocolate is almost completely melted. Meanwhile, beat the eggs, yolks, and sugar together with an electric mixer. Beat with a paddle until light and thick. Beat the melted chocolate and butter together until creamy; it should be quite warm. Pour in the egg mixture, then quickly beat in the flour, just until combined.
Divide the batter among the molds. (If there is still quite a bit of time before dinner, refrigerate the molds, top shelf of the walk-in; you will then have to bring them back out to get them to room temperature before baking.
Put the molds on a sheet pan, fairly spaced out, bake until the center is still quite soft but the sides are set, approx. 6 minutes.

Chocolate decoration
Chocolate ganache
Dessert plate
Whipped cream

Chocolate Decadence
Yield 64 – 4 cakes

……………………..
24 ea. Eggs
1 cup   Sugar
2 lbs. Butter
4 lbs.   Chocolate
1 ½ Tbsp. Vanilla extract

Chop the chocolate and melt with the butter that has been cut up into chunks over a double boiler.

Line springform pan with plastic wrap

Whip together eggs and sugar.
Fold ingredients to combine, add vanilla.

Bake at 300° F in a water bath until set.
Check it in 20-25 minutes.
Take pans out of oven put in freezer for twenty minutes. Then put in walk-in cooler, top shelf.
To cut you will need: long thin knife, 1 Gallon measuring cup filled with hot water, and paper towels. Carefully cut the cake into 16 servings each. Wipe the knife with paper towel after each cut so as to have nice clean lines.
Garnish whipped cream.

Cheesecake Mousse
Yield 50

……………………….
Compote
4 cups strawberries or raspberries
4 cups Sugar
Combine all ingredients in a pot and cook until the mixture bubbles. Transfer to another container and refrigerate

Mousse
6 lbs. Cream cheese – room temperature
4 cups confectioner's sugar
6 Tbsp. vanilla
4 qts. Heavy cream
2 tsp. salt

With the paddle attachment whisk the 6 lbs of cream cheese. Add confectioner's sugar, vanilla, and 2 tsp. Salt. Use the large mixer. When finished transfer to the largest stainless steel bowl.
In the large mixer whisk the heavy cream until it reaches soft peaks (don't overwhip).
Add the heavy cream to the cream cheese mixture and whip until the mixture is light and airy.
Scoop the mixture into the fantasy glasses, at time of service spoon compote over mousse.

Variations: Raspberry, Strawberry, or Pumpkin cheesecake mousse

Chocolate Bananas Foster
Yield 10
....

7 bananas ½ inch thick sliced diagonally
1¼ cups packed brown sugar
8 Tbsp butter
1 cup heavy cream
4 oz finely chopped chocolate
    1 scoop ice cream

Melt butter in pan, add bananas in one layer. Sprinkle brown sugar over top. Turn bananas once. Don't over cook bananas, remove from pan with slotted spoon. Leave the caramel in the pan, add the heavy cream, heat just to a boil, whisk in chocolate.
Hold everything separately. Plate each dessert as ordered.

Brownie Bombe
Yield 24
....

Prepare brownie mix as directed, bake the brownies on a sheet pan. When done cool on a cooling rack.
While brownies are baking.
Scoop ice cream using the large scoop and put on a rack in the freezer.
Once the ice cream is scooped and in freezer prepare the chocolate ganache.

Ganache
3 lbs. chocolate
24 oz. heavy cream

Chop the chocolate very small. Boil the heavy cream pour over the chocolate stir with a rubber spatula to combine.

Pour or dip the ganache over the ice cream.

Garnish
Whipped cream
Strawberry

Strawberry Shortcake
Yield 40
....

Shortcakes
4 lbs. All-purpose flour
3 ¾ oz. Baking powder (weighed on scale)
2 tsp. Salt
13 oz. Granulated sugar
1 lb. 12 oz. Butter
7 ea. Eggs
18 fl. oz. Milk

EggWash
2 ea. Eggs
¼ cup milk

Sift dry ingredients together, cut butter into 1-inch cubes use a fork to combine into dry ingredients. Whisk together milk and eggs. Stir into the butter and dry ingredient mixture. DO NOT OVERMIX or you will be serving hockey pucks.

Ask chef for the cutter to use.
Cut into 3 – inch circles

Whisk together eggs and milk for egg wash brush tops of shortcakes with egg wash and sprinkle a tiny bit of sugar on top.

Bake at 375°F until lightly browned, approx. 10 minutes.

Berries
4#   Strawberries
¾ cup   Sugar

Slice strawberries, lengthwise, combine with sugar. Put in a covered bowl in the walk-in.

Homemade Whipped Cream
1 quart   heavy cream
1 cup   confectionary sugar
1 tsp.   Vanilla

Mix all ingredients in kitchen Aid with a whip attachment until stiff peaks form.
Serve with one scoop of vanilla ice cream

Tiramisu
Yield 20
....
1 cup sugar
4 cups mascarpone cheese
4 cups whipping cream
1 ½ cups strongly brewed coffee
6 tbsp. coffee Liquer
60 Ladyfingers

Brew coffee, pour into shallow hotel pan, allow to cool.

Wash and set aside the fantasy glasses to be used.

Cream mascarpone and sugar until well combined.

Beat whipping cream, fold into mascarpone mixture. Fold in liquer

Soak ladyfingers in strongly brewed coffee.
Place in serving dish
Scoop mascarpone mixture on top

Prepare garnish: chocolate shavings
Serve with whipped cream and chocolate shavings

White Chocolate Mousse and Raspberry Trifle
Yield 35
....

4 cups	white chocolate, chopped
3 Tbsp.	butter
4 cups	mascarpone cheese
2 cups	heavy cream
6 cups	frozen raspberries
3 cups	sugar, divided
1 tbsp.	vanilla extract
½ cup	confectioner's sugar

½ batch yellow cake mix – bake on a sheet pan covered with parchment paper
Follow directions for yellow cake mix. Bake.
Melt white chocolate chips with 3 tbsp. butter over a double boiler.
Measure raspberries and 2 cups sugar, combine and heat on stove until sugar is dissolved. Cool.

Combine mascarpone and 1 cup sugar in kitchen aid mixer. Leave out at room temperature
Whip heavy cream and confectioner's sugar until firm, refrigerate until needed.
For mousse, combine white chocolate and butter with mascarpone sugar mixture, and heavy cream. Refrigerate.
Cut cake into ½ inch cubes.

To build trifle use martini glasses.
Put cake squares on bottom, cover with raspberries, then mousse.

Apple Crisp
Yield 40

………………

48 cups sliced apples
4 Tbsp. cinnamon
3 lemons, juiced
4 ½ cups firmly packed brown sugar
4 cups oats
4 cups flour
1 tsp salt
1 ¼ pounds of butter
¼ cup to ½ cup sugar

Preheat oven to 350 º F. Toss the apples with the granulated sugar, half the cinnamon, and the lemon juice. Divide into the dishes. Top each one with a bit of butter.

Combine all the other ingredients, until you have a crumble like texture.

Spread the topping over the apples bake for 20 minutes or until topping is brown and apples are tender.

Homemade Whipped Cream

………………………………

1 quart   heavy cream
1 cup   confectionary sugar
1 tsp.   Vanilla

Mix all ingredients in kitchen Aid with a whip attachment until stiff peaks form.
Make the whipped cream closer to the time of service so it doesn't fall.

Additional items required: pastry bag and tip

Individual Vanilla Cheesecakes
Yield 24
....

2lb. 12 oz	Cream cheese, room temperature
20 oz.	Granulated Sugar
10 each	Eggs
2 lb. 14 oz.	Sour cream
1 ½ tbsp.	Vanilla extract

Butter 24 - 2 ½ inch ramekins and set them on a sheet pan.

Blend the cream cheese and sugar in the bowl of the kitchen aid mixer fitted with a paddle on low speed until thoroughly combined. Scrape down the bowl and blend on low another minute until well blended.

Add the eggs a small amount at a time, scraping down the bowl and paddle after each addition. **This step is extremely important, make sure to scrape it down otherwise you will have lumps… you do not want lumps.**

Add the sour cream and vanilla.

Pour the smooth batter into the prepared ramekins.

Place sheet pan in a 300 degree F oven. Use the convection oven. Fill the sheet pan with water to create a water bath. (This is to prevent cracking and the cheesecakes coming out looking like soufflé). Bake until set but not cracked on the surface, approximately 30 minutes.

Remove from the water bath and chill immediately after removal from oven. This step is also important if we are to have these cheesecakes cooled before service.

Appendix

Common Units of Measure

Weights and Measure *for water and some liquids*

1 gallon = 4 quarts or 16 cups or 128 fluid ounces

1 quart = 2 pints or 4 cups or 32 fluid ounces

1 pint = 2 cups or 16 fluid ounces

1 cup = 16 tablespoons or 8 fluid ounces

1 Tablespoon = 3 teaspoons or ½ fluid ounce

2 Tablespoons = 1 fluid ounce

Ladles, Spoons, and Scoops

Cup Size		Ladles
¼ cup	=	2 ounces
½ cup	=	4 ounces
¾ cup	=	6 ounces
1 cup	=	8 ounces

Scoop Size		Ounces		Level Measure
#6	=	5 ounces	=	2/3 cup
#8	=	4 ounces	=	½ cup
#10	=	3 ¼ ounces	=	3/8 cup
#12	=	2 ¾ ounce	=	1/3 cup
#16	=	2 ounces	=	¼ cup
#20	=	1 ½ ounce	=	3 ½ Tablespoon
#24	=	1 1/3 ounce	=	2 2/3 Tablespoon
#30	=	1 ounce	=	2 1/5 Tablespoon
#40	=	.8 ounce	=	1 3/5 Tablespoon

NOTE: Scoop number refers to the number of scoops in a quart.

Food Equivalents

1 pound butter	2 cups
1 pound flour	4 cups
1 pound granulated sugar	2 cups
1 pound confectioner's sugar	3 ½ cups
1 pound cornstarch	3 cups
1 ounce salt	2 Tablespoons
1 ounce ground spice	¼ cup
1 pound dry bread crumbs	5 cups
1 pound soft bread crumbs	2 ½ quarts
1 crate whole eggs	30 dozen
5 whole eggs	1 cup
8 egg whites	1 cup
12 egg yolks	1 cup
1 pound brown sugar	2 ¼ - 3 cups
1 ounce flavoring and extracts	2 Tablespoons
1 ounce plain gelatin	3 Tablespoons
3 ounces flavored gelatin	½ cup
8 ounces lemon juice	1 cup (6 lemons)
5 1/3 ounces large marshmallows	1 cup (15 count)
5 1/3 ounce miniature marshmallows	1 cup (87 count)
1 pound nut meats, walnuts, pecans	4 cups
1 pound oats, rolled	5 cups
1 pound chopped onions	2 to 3 cups
4 ounces green pepper chopped	1 cup
1 pound whole green peppers	6
7 ounces pimento, canned, drained, chopped	1 cup
1 pound potatoes	3 medium
1 pound rice, raw	2 cups
1 pound rice, cooked	6 cups
1 ounce baking soda	2 1/3 Tablespoon
1 ounce baking powder	2 ½ Tablespoon
1 pound bananas	3 count
1 pound beef, cooked, diced	3 cups
1 pound loaf bread, sliced	12 to 16 slices
1 pound cabbage	½ small head – 4c. shredded
1 pound celery, diced, raw	2 cups
1 pound cheese, American, grated or ground	4 cups
1 pound cheese, cottage	2 cups
1 ounce baking chocolate	1 square
8 ounces cocoa	2 cups
1 pound cornmeal of Farina	3 cups
1 ounce cornstarch	3 ½ Tablespoons
1 pound graham crackers	66 count, 15= 1 cup crumbs
½ pint heavy cream	1 pint whipped

Performance Evaluation

Your Name:
Student Name:

This evaluation should be completed on your management night or the day after.
Specific, reflective, and **thorough comments** should be added.

5 -Excellent – no improvements can be made
4 -Above average
3 -Average/ ok
2 -Below Average
1 -Needs Vast Improvement

Categories Observed	Score	Comments
Attendance	(1-5)	
Student arrived on time and prepared for class.		
Initiative/ Effort	(1-5)	
The ability and willingness to do what is necessary and go above and beyond without being asked or reminded.		
Work Habits	(1-5)	
Considers safety of work habits, sanitation practices and good housekeeping in work area.		
Attitude	(1-5)	
Person's general attitude toward his/her job, total meal, fellow students.		
Uniform	(1-5)	
Student is dressed in proper uniform as stated in the lab guide.		

TOTAL SCORE out of 25	

Other Observations:

Commonly Used Ingredient Prices

Item	Cost
Bacon	3.30 / lb.
Fish Base	.30 / lb.
Broccoli	.99/ head or 26.20 per case
Butter	3.67 lb.
Celery	1.13/ ea.
Cheddar cheese	5.99/lb.
Cream Cheese	2.03/lb.
Mozzarella cheese (shredded)	3.16/ lb.
Parmesan cheese (grated)	3.20/lb.
Parmesan cheese (shredded)	4.00/lb.
Ricotta cheese	1.53/lb.
Cooking wine (white)	5.88/gal. r .
Cooking wine (sherry)	7.15/gal
Heavy cream	3.07/qt.
Half and half	3.00/ qt.
Sour cream	3.21/lb.
Phyllo dough	2.23/lb
Eggplants	1.32/lb.
Flour (all purpose)	.85/lb.
Garlic	3.65/lb.
Ginger	2.90/lb.
Horseradish	5.10/qt.
Ketchup (bottle)	.15/oz.
Leeks	2.90/bunch
Lemons	4.25/doz.
Mayonnaise	6.75/gal.
Milk	3.38/gal.
Mint	1.15/oz.
Mushrooms (white)	3.00/lb.
Mushrooms (portabella)	5.00/lb.
Mustard (Dijon)	6.20/gal.
Oil (Canola)	9.90/Gal
Oil (olive)	25.74/gal.

Item	Cost
Oil (fryer)	14.95/ box
Onions Red Medium	.73/ .lb
Onions (Scallion)	.53/ bunch
Onions (Spanish, jumbo)	.79 .lb
Parsley	1.00/ bunch
Pasta (Fettuccine)	1.00/ .lb
Pasta (Penne)	1.00/ .lb
Peppers (Green)	2.00 / .lb
Peppers (red)	2.50/ .lb
Rosemary (fresh)	1.45/ .oz
Sage (fresh)	1.10/ .oz
Salmon fillet 6 oz	2.55/ each
Salmon fillet 8 oz	3.44/ each
Sauce (demi glace) concentrate	4.85/ each
Sauce tomato base	4.41/ # 10 can
Shallots	1.80/ .lb
Shrimp 16/20	6.16/ .lb
Spices	
Bay leaves	3.90/ .oz
Cinnamon	.48/ .oz
Garlic Powder	.43/ .oz
Marjoram	1.78/ .oz
Black Pepper	.53/ .oz
Red Pepper	.63/ .oz
White Pepper	.84/ .oz
Spinach	3.60/ .lb
Squash (Zucchini)	.70/ .lb
Thyme Fresh	1.15/ .oz
Tomatoes Diced	3.71/ #10 can
Tomatoes (plum)	1.74/ .lb
Vinegar (Balsamic)	.21/ .oz

Definitions

Á La Carte   1. A menu on which each food and beverage listed and priced separately:
   2. Foods cooked to order as opposed to foods cooked in advance and held for later service.
Albumen – The principle protein found in egg whites.
Al Denté– (al den-tay) Cooked foods, usually vegetables and pasta, that are prepared firm to the bite, not soft or mushy.
Allemande – A sauce made by adding lemon juice and a liaison to a velouté made from veal or chicken stock.
Anthocyanins – Red or purple pigments in vegetables and fruits.
Appetizers – Also known as the first courses, usually small portions of hot or cold foods intended to whet the appetite in anticipation of the more substantial courses to follow.
Au Gratin- Foods made with a browned or crusted top; often made by browning a food with a bread crumb, cheese, and/or sauce topping under a broiler or salamander.
Au Jus (ah zhew) Roast meats, poultry or game served with their natural, unthickened juices.
Bain-marie – Hot or cold water bath used to cook food (double boiler); To keep food warm (steam table); or to keep food cold.
Barding – Tying thin slices of fat, such as bacon over meats or poultry that have little or no natural fats covering it in order to protect and moisten them during roasting.
Baste – To moisten meat while cooking to prevent drying and to add flavor. The liquid used is usually pan drippings, water, or water and fat.
Batonnet - -foods cut into matchstick shapes of ¼ X ¼ inch X 2 ½ inches.
Bay leaf – the aromatic leaves of the sweet-bay or laurel tree grown in the Mediterranean countries and in southern sections of the U.S. Used for seasoning soups, sauces, etc.
Bearnaise - A French cream sauce made with chopped parsley or chervil, tarragon, vinegar, butter, shallots, and egg yolks.
Beurre manie – A combination of equal amounts by weight of flour and soft, whole butter, it is whisked into a simmering sauce at the end of the cooking process for quick thickening and added sheen and flavor.
Binding – Usually applied to the thickening of soups with flour mixed with liquid or fat to prevent separation of ingredients.
Bisque – A thick sauce or soup form shell fish or game.
Blanch - to scald or parboil in water or steam in order to remove the skin from or soften.
Boil – To subject to the action of the heat of boiling liquid, as in especially water.
Bordelaise – A sauce with a reduced meat stock base, beef with Bordeaux wine as its foundation with various seasonings added, such as parsley and diced marrow.
Bouquet Garni – A few herbs, usually a bay leaf with a sprig of parsley, some thyme tied with butchers twine to flavor a soups and sauces (looks like a bouquet of flowers) – may be used in place of a sachet. Remove before serving.
Braise – To brown meat in a hot receptacle in a small amount of fat, then cook slowly in juices from the meat or in added liquid in a covered pan. The added liquid may be water or stock.
Broil – To cook by radiant (direct) heat from a gas flame, or electric element.
Chiffonade – To finely slice or shred leafy vegetables or herbs.
China Cap – A cone shaped strainer made of perforated metal

Clarified Butter – Purified butterfat obtained by melting the butter and removing the water and milk solids.

Deep Frying - A dry heat cooking method using convection to transfer heat to a food submerged in hot fat. Foods to be deep fried are usually first coated in batter or breading.

Deglaze - To swirl or stir a liquid, usually wine or stock, in a sauté pan or other pan to dissolve cooked food particles remaining on the bottom. The resulting mixture often becomes the base for a sauce.

Demitasse – Literally French for "half-cup" can refer to the small coffee cup or the strong black coffee served in the cup.

Emulsification - The process by which generally unmixable liquids, such as oil and water, are forced into a uniform distribution.

Filet – Strips cut from the underside of the loin of beef or mutton and boned.

Fillets – boneless fish

Folding – A mixing method used to gently incorporate light, airy products into heavier ingredients, i.e. mixing dry ingredients with whipped eggs.

Gourmet – a connoisseur of fine food, one with a discriminating palate, 2. a type of restaurant that serves well prepared dishes that are artfully presented.

Hollandaise - A much used warm emulsion sauce of butter, lemon juice, egg yolks and seasonings used with boiled fish, vegetables, eggs benedict, etc.

IQF (Individually Quick Frozen) the technique of rapidly freezing each individual item of food such as slices of fruit, or meats and other items before packaging.

Julienne – to cut vegetables into stick-shaped pieces 1/8 inch X 1/8 X 1 to 2 inches.

Kneading – Working dough to develop the gluten.

Mignon - Tenderloin muscle which is tender in all grades of meat.

Mince – To cut into very small pieces.

Mise en place – literally "everything in its place". It refers to the assembly of all necessary ingredients and equipment.

Parchment paper – A heat resistant paper sued throughout the kitchen for tasks such as lining baking pans, wrapping foods to be cooked 'en papillote'.

Pilaf – A cooking method for gains in which the grains are lightly sautéed in hot fat and then a hot liquid is added. The mixture is simmered without stirring until the liquid is absorbed.

Provencal – a term used to describe dishes served in the style of Provence, a southeastern France region. Usually tomatoes and olive oil are a main part of the dish.

Ramekin – a small, oven proof dish, usually ceramic.

Roux – an equal mixture of butter or other fat and flour, sued for thickening soups and sauces.

Sachet - A few herbs, usually a bay leaf with a sprig of parsley, some thyme, marjoram, sage, black peppercorns, tied in cheesecloth and added to soups and sauces for flavoring. Remove the satchel before serving.

Scalloppine – Thin, *scallop* pieces of meat, dredged in flour, sautéed brown. Served with sauces based on tomatoes or wine.

Mystery Shopper Report

Mystery shopping reports can serve as an important way to identify what you staff is doing right and provide insights into what you and your managers may be missing or where improvements need to be made. The key to maintaining a successful restaurant isn't just attracting first-time customers, it's even more important to create loyal guests who come back again and again. Regularly employing mystery shoppers can help you identify things that are going on in your restaurant that may be causing people to leave and not return. Some restaurants use trained mystery shoppers from firms specializing in this service. Others elect to recruit shoppers from their own pool of friends, acquaintances and even regular customers. Your analysis should be thorough, and specific. **Please evaluate a full service restaurant.**

Fill this report in **completely and thoroughly.**

Your Name _____ Date of Visit _____ # in Party _____
Restaurant Name _____ Server's Name _____
Manager on Duty _____ Day of Week _____ Meal Period _____

CATEGORY	POINTS EARNED	POSSIBLE POINTS	PERCENT
Facility/ Environment		125	
Service/ Personnel		175	
Food & Beverage		50	
TOTALS		**350**	

COMMENTS:
The 3 top things this restaurant did very well:
1. _____

2. _____

3. _____

The 3 top things that could be improved:
1. _____

2. _____

3. _____

Overall comments/observations:
_____

_____

_____

_____

Evaluation continued on next page.

Shoppers Scorecard

Use the scale below to rate your experience and observations in each of the areas detailed below. Total possible points for each item is 5 points. A "5" indicates you observed an outstanding job, a "3" is average and a "1" means poor.

5- Outstanding   4- Above Average   3- Average   2- Below Average   1- Poor

	POINTS	COMMENTS
FACILITY / ENVIRONMENT		
Exterior:		
Parking lot is clean.		
Parking lot spaces clearly marked.		
Driveway and sidewalks free of debris.		
Signs and lights are on and functioning.		
Landscaping is neat and well-kept.		
Flower beds free of weeds and debris.		
Entry door, including windows, are clean.		
Front Entrance:		
Lobby is neat and orderly.		
Hostess stand is neat and orderly.		
All light fixtures are working.		
Dining Room:		
Windows are clean.		
Floors clean and free of stains and excessive wear.		
Table spotless when seated.		
Staff uniforms clean, neat and attractive.		
Condiments and table top items clean and in order.		
Light fixtures free of dust, dirt and spots.		
Chairs and seats clean and free of food particles.		
Booth frames, window sills and other Surfaces clean and polished.		
Restrooms:		
Restrooms are odor-free		
Floors are clean and free of dirt, water and trash.		
Urinals/toilets clean and odor-free.		
Sinks, fixtures, counters and mirrors clean and polished.		
Soap dispensers clean and working properly.		
Supplies in adequate supply (soap, paper towels, toilet paper).		
Trash receptacles emptied to prevent overflow of paper towels.		
CATEGORTY SCORE		

Comments on Facility Environment _____

SERVICE / PERSONNEL **Host / Hostess:**	POINTS	COMMENTS
Greeted and welcomed with a smile.		
Friendly demeanor. Positive interaction with guests.		
Asked for table preference.		
Received accurate wait time.		
Telephone answered promptly.		
Seated efficiently and courteously.		
Asked if table was OK while being seated.		
Menus handed to guests, not placed on the table.		
Departing guests recognized and thanked.		
Dining Room: Promptly greeted by server(within 60 secs. with smile.)		
Pleasant, friendly and personable demeanor. Good eye contact.		
Description of house/daily specialties offered.		
Server showed knowledge of menu items.		
Server made appropriate suggestions (beverages, appetizers, specialty coffees, dessert).		
Orders taken when ready.		
Salads, appetizers served within 7 minutes of order.		
Entrees served within 12 minutes of order.		
Person delivering food knows who gets what.		
Within 5 minutes after entrée delivered, server checked back to ask about food.		
All reasonable requests accommodated – even off-menu		
Beverages refilled in a timely manner.		
Owner or manager on the floor.		
Check presented promptly.		
Change, receipt returned promptly.		
Thanked by server and invited to return.		
BAR: Greeted within 60 seconds – beverages napkin set.		
Bartender/ server friendly, encourages positive interaction.		
Specialty drinks recommended.		
Order taken and drinks served promptly.		
No employee observed drinking, eating or engaged in personal conversations.		
All orders recorded on register.		
Guest checks presented to guests promptly when tabs are run.		
Thanked by bartender/server and invited to return.		
CATEGORY SCORE		

Service/PersonnelComments_____

_____

FOOD & BEVERAGE	POINTS	COMMENTS
Attractive plate presentation.		
Adequate variety and price points.		
Portion sizes appropriate, not too big or too small.		
Hot food served hot, cold food served cold.		
Appetizer tasty and served as ordered.		
Salad ingredients fresh, tasty and served as ordered.		
Entrees tasty and served as ordered. Note entrees selected.		
Desserts tasty and served as ordered.		
Beverages tasty and served as ordered.		
Good price / value relationship.		
CATEGORTY SCORE		

Food and Beverage Comments _____
_____
_____
_____

Overall comments _____
_____
_____
_____
_____
_____